DATE DUE

NoLex 10|12

MAO ZEDONG

C.J. Shane, *Book Editor*

Daniel Leone, *President*
Bonnie Szumski, *Publisher*
Scott Barbour, *Managing Editor*
David M. Haugen, *Series Editor*

GREENHAVEN
PRESS®

THOMSON
™
GALE

San Diego • Detroit • New York • San Francisco • Cleveland
New Haven, Conn. • Waterville, Maine • London • Munich

For more information, contact
Greenhaven Press
27500 Drake Rd.
Farmington Hills, MI 48331-3535
Or you can visit our Internet site at http://www.gale.com

LIBRARY OF CONGRESS CATALOGING-IN-PUBLICATION DATA

Mao Zedong / C.J. Shane, book editor.
   p. cm. — (People who made history)
Includes bibliographical references and index.
ISBN 0-7377-1494-8 (pbk. : alk. paper) —
ISBN 0-7377-1493-X (lib. bdg. : alk. paper)
   1. Zedong, Mao, 1893–1976. 2. China—Politics and government—1949– .
I. Shane, C.J. II. Series.
DS778.M3M28524 2004
951.05'092—dc21   2003044855

Printed in the United States of America

CONTENTS

Leap Forward. When extreme leftist elements came forward, Mao encouraged them and called for a renewal of revolutionary values. The result was the Cultural Revolution, a period of chaos and murderous purges that has been called China's "ten years of madness."

FOREWORD

In the vast and colorful pageant of human history, a handful of individuals stand out. They are the men and women who have come variously to be called "great," "leading," "brilliant," "pivotal," or "infamous" because they and their deeds forever changed their own society or the world as a whole. Some were political or military leaders—kings, queens, presidents, generals, and the like—whose policies, conquests, or innovations reshaped the maps and futures of countries and entire continents. Among those falling into this category were the formidable Roman statesman/general Julius Caesar, who extended Rome's power into Gaul (what is now France); Caesar's lover and ally, the notorious Egyptian queen Cleopatra, who challenged the strongest male rulers of her day; and England's stalwart Queen Elizabeth I, whose defeat of the mighty Spanish Armada saved England from subjugation.

Some of history's other movers and shakers were scientists or other thinkers whose ideas and discoveries altered the way people conduct their everyday lives or view themselves and their place in nature. The electric light and other remarkable inventions of Thomas Edison, for example, revolutionized almost every aspect of home-life and the workplace; and the theories of naturalist Charles Darwin lit the way for biologists and other scientists in their ongoing efforts to understand the origins of living things, including human beings.

Still other people who made history were religious leaders and social reformers. The struggles of the Arabic prophet Muhammad more than a thousand years ago led to the establishment of one of the world's great religions—Islam; and the efforts and personal sacrifices of an American reverend named Martin Luther King Jr. brought about major improvements in race relations and the justice system in the United States.

Each anthology in the People Who Made History series begins with an introductory essay that provides a general overview of the individual's life, times, and contributions. The group of essays that follow are chosen for their accessibility to a young adult audience and carefully edited in consideration of the reading and comprehension levels of that audience. Some of the essays are by noted historians, professors, and other experts. Others are excerpts from contemporary writings by or about the pivotal individual in question. To aid the reader in choosing the material of immediate interest or need, an annotated table of contents summarizes the article's main themes and insights.

Each volume also contains extensive research tools, including a collection of excerpts from primary source documents pertaining to the individual under discussion. The volumes are rounded out with an extensive bibliography and a comprehensive index.

Plutarch, the renowned first-century Greek biographer and moralist, crystallized the idea behind Greenhaven's People Who Made History when he said, "To be ignorant of the lives of the most celebrated men of past ages is to continue in a state of childhood all our days." Indeed, since it is people who make history, every modern nation, organization, institution, invention, artifact, and idea is the result of the diligent efforts of one or more individuals, living or dead; and it is therefore impossible to understand how the world we live in came to be without examining the contributions of these individuals.

INTRODUCTION

Historians describe Mao Zedong both as a visionary and a tyrant. He unified a war-torn China and consistently promoted the rights and welfare of the common people. He also was responsible for the deaths of millions by starvation and execution. Although the historical assessment of Mao continues, most historians agree that Mao was a man who achieved both great successes and great failures in his decades-long rule.

PEASANT CHILDHOOD

Mao Zedong was born in 1893, in the Year of the Snake according to the Chinese lunar calendar. He was the oldest child in a moderately prosperous peasant family in the village of Shaoshan in Hunan Province. Mao's mother, Wen Qimei, was illiterate, but Mao remembered her as kindhearted and generous. Mao's father, Mao Shunsheng, had only two years of schooling, yet he was a hardworking and ambitious man who used his limited resources to increase the family wealth. His father was also a demanding and hot-tempered man who often beat his sons. In 1936 Mao Zedong told American journalist Edgar Snow that he viewed his father as a tyrant and a bully, and Mao learned early to rebel against the father he hated.

Historian Dick Wilson sees in this father-son relationship the origins of Mao's identification with downtrodden Chinese peasants who were trapped in a similar relationship to a despotic emperor. "The energy that drove [Mao] was hatred of the fiercest kind, derived from his personal sense of rejection. . . . Mao was not merely angry because he felt himself unloved: he identified with the peasantry in their rejection by the Chinese elite, by the Chinese tradition, by the Chinese system."[1]

Historian Lee Feigon suggests that Mao may have overstated the hostility between himself and his father. "Stories of

8

youthful rebellion against one's family and tales of horrible fathers were wildly popular among young Chinese intellectuals at the time Edgar Snow first interviewed Mao,"² says Feigon.

After finishing primary school, Mao asked to continue his education, but his father wanted the boy back at work on the family farm. To tie down his rebellious son, Mao's father arranged for Mao to be married at the age of fourteen to a girl four years his senior. Mao insisted later that he did not want the marriage and never lived with the girl as husband and wife, although there is evidence that he actually did live with her. After his wife's death, Mao left home in 1911. He told everyone that he was off to seek more education. At first Mao's father resisted, but he eventually gave in and paid for Mao's tuition at a new school.

EARLY INFLUENCES ON MAO

A famine occurred in the region during Mao's student years. When hungry peasants tried to seize his family's grain, the young Mao felt compassion for their distress yet disapproved of the peasants' willingness to use violence to get the grain. When the starving peasants rioted, imperial officials punished them and beheaded their leaders. Mao told Edgar Snow, "I never forgot it. I felt that there with the rebels were ordinary people like my own family and I deeply resented the injustice of the treatment given to them."³

This lifelong concern for the Chinese peasant was an important theme in Mao's life. Another theme was Mao's patriotism and anti-imperialism. He was deeply influenced by books and articles sent to him by his cousin that called for fundamental changes in Chinese government and society. These readings increased Mao's desire for more education, so in 1911 he traveled to the Hunan provincial capital of Changsha to enter a new school. A few weeks later revolution broke out in Wuhan, a city in central China.

The revolutionary movement was led by Sun Yat-sen (1866–1925), a physician from southern China. Mao was inspired by Sun's revolutionary movement to replace the imperial Qing dynasty with a democratic government. Mao joined the army and served until it was clear that the Qing emperor had been overthrown. Then Mao returned to Changsha to continue his studies. After months spending most of his time reading in the public library, he enrolled at the Hunan Normal School. For five years, Mao studied there to be a teacher and graduated in 1918 at the age of twenty-four.

As a student, Mao was profoundly influenced by his ethics professor, Yang Changji. Yang was a brilliant scholar and a participant in the New Culture Movement sweeping China. Despite the political chaos of the times—the central government was weak, and China was ruled by regional warlords— the intellectual and cultural life of the nation was undergoing a renaissance. Leaders of the New Culture Movement rejected traditional Confucian values that they damned as "feudal." New Culture leaders advocated a turn to science, democracy, and to educational and social reforms in the search to modernize China. New political philosophies emerged and were debated as well.

Under Yang's guidance, Mao began developing his own philosophy. He wrote a paper on the importance of physical exercise that was published in *New Youth*, a leading journal of the New Culture Movement. Mao also helped create the New People's Study Society, a group dedicated to studying the modernization of China.

As a student in Changsha, Mao began a practice that he continued throughout his life—promoting education for the poor. He founded a night school in Changsha for adult peasants and workers, where he taught literacy and math.

When Professor Yang moved to Beijing to take a prestigious position at Beijing University in 1918, Mao followed him. Yang helped Mao get a job as a clerk in the university library, where Mao came in contact with leaders of the New Culture Movement. They largely ignored Mao. "They had no time to listen to an assistant librarian speaking southern dialect,"[4] Mao said. He was lonely in Beijing, but Mao was exposed to many new and exciting ideas, including a new political philosophy called Marxism. He also had time to visit Professor Yang's daughter, Yang Kaihui (1901–1930), with whom he was becoming quite attached.

When his mother became ill, Mao left Beijing to return home. He was not in Beijing on May 4, 1919, when students took to the streets to protest foreign imperialism. The protests formed in response to proposals made at the Versailles Peace Conference at the end of World War I. One of the outcomes of the peace conference was to transfer German-controlled territory in Shandong Province to Japan instead of returning it to China. Growing Chinese nationalist sentiment made this violation of their territorial rights unacceptable. Many leaders of the New Culture Movement aligned themselves with the May Fourth anti-imperialism movement, and the two movements are commonly linked in history texts.

LIFE AS A TEACHER AND WRITER

Mao's beloved mother died in 1919. Rather than return to Beijing, Mao found a teaching position in Changsha. He had absorbed many new ideas from the leaders of the New Culture Movement while in Beijing. Now Mao brought these ideas home to Hunan Province. He lectured and wrote on New Culture themes, and he published a journal that was suppressed by Hunan's ruling warlord, Zhang Jingyao. Mao also founded a Marxist study society in Changsha and organized a student strike against the warlord. Again, Mao founded a night school for adults and insisted on including peasants in his classes.

Like other members of the New Culture Movement, Mao became a strong advocate for women's rights. He wrote a series of articles about the suicide of a Miss Zhao, a Chinese woman who killed herself rather than enter an arranged marriage. Mao condemned the system of forced marriages and argued that marriage should be based on love. Mao began a serious critique of all tyrannical government institutions, and in August 1919 he wrote "The Great Union of the Popular Masses," in which, for the first time, he named aristocrats and capitalists as enemies of the people. He now believed that only revolution would benefit China.

Mao returned briefly to Beijing to see Yang Changji just before his old professor died. Mao's father died shortly after Yang's death. Alone now, Mao returned to Changsha. The warlord Zhang had been overthrown, and Mao felt free to establish a business, the Cultural Book Society, which became quite successful. Mao's holdings included several bookstores and a publishing house dedicated to socialism and other radical ideas. Mao also began living with his old professor's daughter, Yang Kaihui, who had returned to Changsha after her father's death. The two later married and she eventually gave birth to three sons, Mao Anying (1922–1951), Mao Anqing (1923–), and Mao Anlong (1927–1931).

By late 1920, at the age of twenty-seven, Mao had become a successful businessman, teacher, writer, political activist, and family man. After an early interest in anarchist theory, he settled on Marxist socialism as the answer to China's problems. Socialism was a political philosophy that advocated communal (Communist) ownership of resources by all the people, not by a few individuals. Having made Marxism his political philosophy, Mao dedicated his life to seeing that China would become a Communist state.

THE COMMUNIST PARTY AND THE GUOMINDANG

By 1920 Russian Communists began sending agents abroad to guide the development of communism in other countries, including China. These international agents came to be known as the Comintern. The Comintern advisers invited Mao and other Chinese Marxists to a secret meeting in Shanghai in 1921. The Chinese Communist Party (CCP) was established at this meeting.

From the beginning, Chinese Communists had two problems. The first was fitting Marxist theory to the Chinese situation. Karl Marx claimed that the urban working class (the proletariat) was the primary force that would bring about revolutionary change. Mao realized that it would be rural peasants, not urban workers, who would lead China's revolution.

The second problem was what to do about the Guomindang, the Nationalist Party that had been founded by Sun Yat-sen. The Guomindang, now led by Chiang Kai-shek (1887–1975), was a party devoted to Chinese nationalism, but it was not Communist. Still, Chinese Communist Party members, under orders from the Comintern, joined with the Guomindang in a united front to subdue the remaining Chinese warlords.

Agreeing with these common goals, Mao spent the next few years as an officer of both the Guomindang and the CCP. He organized strikes, wrote articles, and spoke on behalf of alliance goals. He also continued to speak on the revolutionary potential of China's peasantry, and he promoted peasant needs and concerns. He traveled often, and he had little time to be with Yang Kaihui and their sons.

In an article published in 1925, Mao introduced the idea of the Chinese peasant ("rural proletariat") as a revolutionary force. According to Lee Feigon, Mao argued that the peasants "hoped to eliminate warlords, bullies and bad landlords. They wanted famine relief for the unemployed and better treatment of young farm laborers and women workers. They aimed to forbid usurious loans, reduce working hours, and abolish exorbitant taxes. Finally, they wanted adult education classes."[5] In 1927 Mao published one of his most famous tracts, "The Report on the Peasant Movement in Hunan," based on a detailed study he did of peasants in his home province. In response to harsh living conditions, the peasants took matters into their own hands, formed revolutionary groups, and overthrew their local landlords. Mao was passionately enthusiastic about their efforts.

RETREAT TO THE MOUNTAINS

Guomindang general Chiang Kai-shek, supported by the Communists, led his troops against China's warlords and subdued them. Chiang then turned on his Communist allies. Fearful of growing Communist influence, Chiang launched a vicious attack on Communists in Shanghai and other cities in 1927. In Shanghai alone, five thousand Communists were slaughtered.

The surviving CCP membership met in an emergency conference at which Mao and others argued for the establishment of a military force to fight back. "Political power is obtained out of the barrel of a gun,"[6] Mao said, noting that Chiang Kai-shek's success was due to his willingness to use force. Zhu De, a Communist military leader, pulled together the first troops in what came to be known as the Red Army. In 1928 the CCP Central Committee ordered Mao to lead some Red Army troops against the Guomindang using conventional military tactics, not the guerrilla strategy Mao preferred. His troops were swiftly defeated in what was called the Autumn Harvest Uprising. Mao was captured, but he quickly managed to escape.

Mao and his comrades fled to an isolated stronghold in the Jinggang Mountains on the border between Hunan and Jiangxi provinces. Zhu De (1886–1976) and another Communist military leader, Peng Dehuai (1898–1974), and their troops later joined Mao in the mountain retreat. Secure within the province, the Communists established a land reform program that involved confiscating land from wealthy men in the region and redistributing it to peasants. Ever the teacher, Mao also set about educating his old followers as well as the curious peasants in the principles of Marxism.

For months now, Mao had been separated from Yang Kaihui and their three sons. In his mountain retreat, he became lovers with an ardent and strong-willed young Communist named He Zizhen (1909–1984). Philip Short says of this union, "[Mao's] decision to take the young woman as his partner seems to have been an almost conscious step in a gradual cutting of the ties that bound him to the world outside, the 'normal' world that had been his before the revolution claimed him."[7] Mao and He Zizhen's first child was born in 1929.

Mao's wife and sons did not fare well in Mao's absence. Yang Kaihui was captured in 1930 by a local warlord, who demanded that she denounce her husband. Yang Kaihui refused, and she was executed on the spot. Friends secretly carried off Mao's three young sons and hid them in Shanghai. The youngest died of dysentery there, but the older boys survived by living on the streets. When Mao Zedong heard of Yang Kaihui's death, he mourned for a short time, then married He Zizhen.

By this time, Mao was out of favor with the CCP leadership. Central Committee members did not like his independence and autonomy, or his advocacy of guerrilla warfare tactics that they considered overly cautious. They disagreed with his continued insistence that peasants, not urban workers, were China's most important revolutionary force.

THE JIANGXI SOVIET

Pursued by the Guomindang, Mao and his comrades fled the mountains in 1929, and he and Zhu De set up a new base near Ruijin on the Fujian-Jiangxi border. There, they established the Jiangxi Soviet, a region of seventeen counties where Socialist principles were put into practice. The soviet was based on the Russian Communist "soviet" controlled by worker councils. Jiangxi was one of nine soviets in China.

For five years, Mao lived at Jiangxi and worked to create a model Socialist state. He conducted additional studies on peasant life in the region, instituted land reform, and established social reforms that gave legal rights to women. He built the Red Army into a disciplined force and required that his troops follow a code of good behavior. Again, he established schools for the peasants and soldiers.

Mao also demonstrated at the Jiangxi Soviet that he was willing to suppress his enemies. In 1930 he arrested nearly four thousand Communist troops and executed about half of those. He claimed that the arrested men were traitors who had ties to the Guomindang.

The political situation for Mao became more difficult when a power struggle developed inside the CCP. One faction of the party leadership included the twenty-eight Bolsheviks, or Moscow-educated Chinese, who were determined to guide China's revolution along Russian lines. Things came to a head when CCP Central Committee members were forced to abandon Shanghai and retreat to the Jiangxi Soviet. There, the CCP leadership transferred powers from Mao to Zhou Enlai (1899–1976) and the Moscow-educated Chinese. Though still technically leader of the soviet, Mao was followed everywhere and may have even been put under house arrest by the pro-Russian faction. Mao also was battling malaria and tuberculosis. Ill and depressed, Mao suffered through the lowest point in his political career.

Meanwhile, Chiang Kai-shek, now receiving Nazi German military aid, pursued the Communists and attacked them again and again in a series of "encirclement campaigns" that tightened the noose on the Jiangxi Soviet. With 1 million troops under his command, Chiang launched the fifth and final campaign in 1933. By the following year, the Jiangxi Soviet shrunk to six of its original seventeen counties.

THE LONG MARCH

In late 1934 the Jiangxi Soviet was far from secure. Historian Jonathan D. Spence explains,

> During this period, the attacks from Chiang Kai-shek's forces became so relentless that the Communist Party leadership decided, secretly, that they would have to abandon their base. Mao was not involved in the planning of this all-important event in Chinese communist history, the first step in what was later to be called 'the Long March.' He and his wife joined the great column of some 86,000 fleeing communist troops and supporters only as it passed near their residence on October 18.[8]

A small garrison was left behind at Jiangxi to cover the escape. One of the men assigned to the garrison was Mao's brother Mao Zetan. He was killed a few months later when the entire region finally fell to the Guomindang. Of the fleeing Communists, only those able to handle the rigors of the journey were allowed to join the retreat. Mao and He Zizhen had to leave behind their small son with a peasant family. Their daughter born in 1929 and a second son born at Jiangxi Soviet had both died in infancy.

Thus began the legendary Long March. The party leadership had no plan other than to escape. They met again at Zunyi in the Guangxi Province in 1935 after a westward trek of over one thousand miles through southern China. At this meeting, Mao began to ascend again in the party power structure. Because he had not been involved in the decision making, Mao could not be blamed for the disastrous policies that led to the destruction of the Jiangxi Soviet. Nor was he responsible for abandoning Jiangxi and for leading the people out in a desperate and aimless march. Mao took over the military conduct of the retreat, and the decisions he made turned out to be key to the marchers' survival.

Doggedly pursued by Guomindang troops, the fleeing Communists turned northward. For the next year, they crossed raging torrents, snowy mountains, impenetrable jungles, and stinking swamps in a journey that would extend to more than six thousand miles. They suffered battle wounds, illness, and starvation, and they were forced to watch as thousands of their comrades died along the way. At one point, Mao's wife, He Zizhen, pregnant again, was wounded in a bombing raid. More than a dozen pieces of shrapnel were still in her body when she gave birth to her fourth child. This infant, too, was left with local peasants when the marchers moved on.

Mao reverted to his preferred guerrilla warfare tactics to stall his pursuers. He used decoys to mislead the Guomindang so that his troops could safely escape traps set at river crossings. Every mile along the way, Mao stayed with his men, talked with them, joked with them, encouraged them, and did what he could to keep up their spirits.

When Mao and his desperate band arrived at the Shaanxi Soviet at Yanan in northern China nearly a year later, the marchers had been reduced from nearly ninety thousand to only about five thousand. Yanan, long a Communist-held region, was a safe haven for the marchers, who had become legends and symbolic of the toughness and determination of the Communist revolutionary. For his part, Mao Zedong had emerged as a heroic figure.

At Yanan

Mao and his wife set up housekeeping in a comfortable furnished cave in a Yanan hillside. The region was poor and arid with few building materials, and cave dwelling was common. He Zizhen cared for a daughter, Li Min, who had been born after the Long March, while awaiting the birth of a sixth child. Mao cared for a small tomato garden and spent hours talking politics with comrades.

Shaanxi Soviet's isolation and poverty made it less vulnerable to Guomindang threats, and the Communists were able to enact social reforms. Land was distributed to peasants, and medical care and education classes were provided as well. The revolutionary spirit fostered at the Yanan encampment made people feel that they were part of a historic movement destined to transform China.

Because of a common concern about the Japanese, who had militarily overtaken Manchuria in northern China, the Chinese Communists decided to set aside their differences. Next, they agreed to enter into a union with the Guomindang and fight the Japanese aggressors together. Guomindang leader Chiang Kai-shek agreed to this second united front in 1937 only because the Japanese army was already at Beijing's doorstep. But even as they stood united against the Japanese, the Communists and the Nationalists did not trust each other. As he had done years before in Shanghai, Chiang even betrayed his Communist allies by sending his troops against one of the Communist armies in 1940. This treachery, however, only convinced many Chinese citizens that Chiang was an unscrupulous leader and actually helped the Communists win new converts to their cause.

Mao began to consolidate his position at Yanan. He found his main rival to be a Marxist theoretician and member of the CCP Politboro named Wang Ming (1904–1974). To counteract Wang's influence, Mao began a systematic study of Marxist writings. He then wrote a series of essays in which he reinterpreted Marxism in a Chinese context. Mao would prove himself able to take the Marxist philosophical concepts and make them practical and applicable to the Chinese situation and to make these concepts understandable to his countrymen. His writings and talks at Yanan became the basis of what would be called "Mao Zedong Thought."

MAO ZEDONG THOUGHT

Mao's philosophy has been summarized by historian John King Fairbank and broken down into three important concepts: "The first principle was party control based on indoctrination of cadres and enforcement of discipline . . . the second principle was to find out what the peasants wanted and give it to them. . . . As these efforts went forward, they became the basis for a third principle: class struggle."[9] "Thought reform" was established to indoctrinate followers and to keep discipline. Thought reform methods included requiring party members to attend intensive study and self-criticism sessions where they were intimidated and humiliated into compliance.

The second principle came to be known as the doctrine of the "mass line." Peasant needs and economic welfare were the first consideration. Edward J. Lazzerini comments,

> Even the doctrine of the "mass line," which encouraged party cadres to maintain direct contact with the masses so as to understand better their concerns, was fundamentally manipulative because it presumed that those "above" the people, with better appreciation of history and theory, would be able to reach the decisions best suited to the people's interests.[10]

Mao's concept of class struggle called on all true revolutionaries to struggle continually against bourgeois revisionists who represented the old hierarchical relationships of feudal China. Land reform was a key element of the class struggle. Lazzerini continues,

> Mao's solution was to disrupt the social networks by encouraging wide-ranging violations of social conventions. Getting peasants to struggle against their landlords who frequently were relatives, or workers against their supervisors, or students against their teachers meant challenging profound taboos about authority and social identity. Giving the people the "right" to struggle was meant to empower them in their relations to authority, impress upon them the rewards of doing so, create a sense of self-reliance in them, and suggest to them that their active involvement in the revolution was critical. In abstract terms, Mao's theories about struggle were attractive to many; in practice their consequences were often economically disastrous and humanly tragic.[11]

At Yanan, Mao conducted a series of lengthy interviews with American journalist Edgar Snow. Snow's portrayal of Mao as a peasant populist inspired both Chinese and Western intellectuals. Yanan began to attract many youthful revolutionaries from China's cities who wanted to participate in the spirit of the times.

Some of the youthful revolutionaries were flirtatious young women. He Zizhen caught Mao with one. The furious He Zizhen hit Mao repeatedly with a flashlight and then attacked the other woman. Mao tried to smooth things over, but the long-suffering He Zizhen wouldn't hear of it. She left Mao. Pregnant again and with her body still studded with shrapnel, she went to the Soviet Union to seek medical treatment. Mao and He Zizhen's sixth child, a boy, was born there but died a few months later of pneumonia. Eventually He Zizhen returned to China a broken woman who suffered from illness and severe depression much of the rest of her life.

Mao then became involved with a twenty-four-year-old Shanghai actress named Jiang Qing (1914–1991), who had joined the troops at Yanan. Soon the two were living together, and their daughter, Li Na, was born in 1940. The party leadership severely criticized Mao for his relationship with Jiang Qing. They told him that he should be patching things up with his wife, He Zizhen, who had proved herself to be a dedicated Communist and a hero of the Long March. To mollify them, Mao promised that he would not allow Jiang Qing to participate in politics. He did not keep this promise. Years later, during the Cultural Revolution, Jiang Qing would become the leader of a radical group known as the Gang of Four.

THE CULT OF MAO AND THE RECTIFICATION CAMPAIGN

A personality cult grew up around Mao during the Yanan years. The peasants at Yanan thought of Mao as a man living a charmed life, one with almost superhuman qualities, who had come to save China.

Mao's supporters contributed to this cult by promoting Mao in a personally flattering manner. Jonathan Spence writes about a portrait of Mao that was published in a Yanan newspaper in 1937:

> Mao was shown full face, with a background of troops under waving banners. Mao's face, in the picture, was illuminated by the rays of the sun, while under the portrait was printed one of his "sayings," calling for the liberation of the Chinese nation and society. In the fall of 1937, young supporters of Mao began to compile a collection of Mao's short works for publication, with an adulatory essay. No Chinese Communist leader's works had ever been published in this way.[12]

To solidify his control over the party, Mao called for thought reform as part of the effort to educate the troops and the party's intellectuals. This was an old idea based on the very ancient Confucian tradition that individuals could be improved through education. Again Mao demonstrated his belief in the value of education, but increasingly Mao insisted that everyone study his own interpretation of Marxism and the principles of Mao Zedong Thought. This push for Socialist education evolved into the Rectification Campaign (1942–1944).

During the Rectification Campaign, individuals were required to engage in constant study and self-criticism, and "reform through education" was promoted. There was intense pressure to conform to the Maoist party line. Those who did not conform were purged. Many were tortured and even executed in an attempt to weed out all dissidents. More than forty thousand individuals were forced out of the CCP. Kang Sheng (1898–1975) was chosen by Mao to be his hatchet man and carry out these purges. Kang, dressed in black clothing and riding a black horse, must have been a terrifying figure to many at Yanan.

Mao's rival, Wang Ming, became a target of rectification. Wang Ming eventually went into exile in the Soviet Union to escape Mao's retribution. Another target was Wang Shiwei, who had written about some of the inequalities that had emerged in Communist society at Yanan. When he refused to admit to any mistake, Wang Shiwei was expelled from the party, arrested, jailed, tortured, and executed. For the many artists and intellectuals at Yanan, Mao reminded them of the role of art in the revolution. Art was not created "for art's sake," Mao said. Art had but one purpose and one purpose only: to serve the people.

WORLD WAR II AND THE WAR OF LIBERATION

In 1939 war had broken out in Europe. Japan, which had been occupying Chinese soil since 1931, now allied with the German Nazis and began implementing its plan to conquer all of Asia. In 1937 the Japanese pushed south from Manchuria into the heartland of China. They took Beijing, then Nanjing, as they drove toward Shanghai. Some of the worst depredations in the history of warfare were committed by the Japanese army against Chinese civilians during this invasion.

The United States came into the war when the Japanese attacked Pearl Harbor, Hawaii, in 1941. Wanting to cooperate with the Chinese to defeat Japan, the United States sent military and financial aid to the Guomindang government, which the United States recognized as the legitimate government of China. Although the United States recommended that the Guomindang cooperate with the CCP and Red Army to bring about a common victory, the United States was growing increasingly suspicious of international commu-

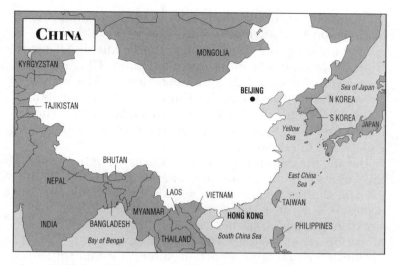

nism in light of a new war that was developing—the Cold War. Chiang Kai-shek vehemently refused to cooperate with the Chinese Communists.

In 1945 Japan surrendered to the United States, and World War II in Asia was over. Mao and Chiang met after the war, and they tried to reach an agreement on rebuilding China, but to no avail. Within months, a civil war broke out between the Guomindang and the Red Army. The United States continued to send aid to the corrupt and ineffectual Guomindang leadership. The Red Army, lean and well disciplined, received aid from the Soviet Union. By 1949 the civil war, referred to today in China as the "war of liberation," was over. Chiang Kai-shek fled to Taiwan and moved his Republic of China government with him. He vowed until his death in 1975 to retake the mainland.

On October 1, 1949, Mao stood at the Gate of Heavenly Peace (Tiananmen), one of the entrances to the Forbidden City, and declared the establishment of the People's Republic of China (PRC) to a cheering crowd. "The Chinese people have stood up,"[13] said Chairman Mao.

BUILDING A NEW NATION

War did not cease during these early years of the People's Republic. A civil war had broken out on the Korean peninsula. Mao ordered Chinese troops to fight on behalf of the North Korean Communist regime, and the United States and United Nations supported the South Korean government.

Thousands of Chinese died in this war, including Mao's beloved son Mao Anying.

Mao also sent the People's Liberation Army into Tibet to consolidate Chinese control over the region. Tibet had long been a vassal region of the Chinese emperors. Mao's interest was to return Tibet to a unified China. The Communists also wanted to liberate the Tibetans from a feudal society. The Tibetans preferred to be ruled by the their religious and political leader, the Dalai Lama.

Despite the continuing warfare, spirits were high among the Chinese people in the early days of the People's Republic. The challenges facing the citizenry were daunting. The economy was in a shambles, and the country's industry, agriculture, and infrastructure had been decimated by years of warfare. Even so, there was great hope.

One of the first of Mao's actions after the establishment of the PRC was to seek further aid from the Soviet Union. The two countries signed a treaty in which the Soviets agreed to give massive technical and financial aid to the Chinese. Mao was strongly influenced by the Soviet Union as a model for building a new China. Soviet-style five-year plans for industrial and agricultural development were instituted, and workers were organized into *danwei*, or work units that provided them with housing and social services. The Chinese education system also followed the Soviet model. A national language, Mandarin Chinese, was adopted, the infrastructure was repaired and expanded, and social reforms were instituted. Anticorruption and antitheft campaigns were established. Crime rates in China dropped dramatically.

At the same time, the Chinese economy developed rapidly. By 1956, only seven years after the establishment of the PRC, the standard of living for the average Chinese citizen had dramatically improved. Life expectancy in China in 1950 was thirty-six years. By 1957, life expectancy had increased to fifty-seven years.

Agriculture was a key aspect of Mao's strategy for economic development. A land reform program was instituted even before the People's Republic was formally established in 1949. Peasants received individual plots of land to work on their own behalf.

One result of the land reform movement was the "settling-of-accounts" movement. In many places, peasants took matters into their own hands and attacked the landlords. Historian J.A.G. Roberts writes, "This resulted in a violent assault on the landlords as a class and led to many deaths—for example, in the village of Long Bow in Shanxi at least a dozen people were beaten to death for having been associated with the system of exploitation."[14] Across China, millions of landlords were murdered in the settling-of-accounts movement.

To Mao, ownership of land by individual peasants was capitalistic, and only an intermediate stage on the way to the goal of communism. He wanted agricultural land to be owned communally by all the people. To that end, Mao pushed for the establishment and expansion of agricultural producer cooperatives (APCs).

Under the APC system, land was pooled and worked collectively by large groups of peasant families. Party officials hoped that the APCs would increase agricultural efficiency, but output was disappointing. Two-thirds of the country had been organized into APCs by the end of 1956. Despite a bumper crop in 1955, agricultural yields continued to be below expectation. Bureaucrats and sometimes the peasants themselves began to dismantle the APCs and return small plots to individual families. Mao viewed this retrenchment as a threat to his goal of communism.

THE HUNDRED FLOWERS

Mao had another problem as well. How could he encourage the intellectuals of Chinese society to make original contributions that would enhance the economic development of the nation? Mao wanted to decrease China's dependence on Soviet technocrats. However, under the constant remolding of Mao's thought reform campaigns, the intellectuals had become demoralized and were unwilling to speak out.

Mao initiated the Hundred Flowers Campaign in 1957 to encourage intellectual participation. One of Mao's goals at the time was to open the CCP bureaucracy to criticism. Mao was convinced that the entrenched party bureaucracy was holding back the nation's development. He hoped that the intellectuals could aid him in his campaign to reduce the bureaucracy's power.

"Let a hundred schools of thought contend," Mao announced, "and let a hundred flowers bloom."[15] This was a reference to a much earlier time in Chinese history, the Hundred Schools era during the Zhou dynasty (1122–256 B.C.), when Confucianism, Daoism, and many other philosophies first appeared. Initially intellectuals were reluctant to answer Mao's call. When thousands did finally step forward, Mao was shocked at the intensity of their criticisms. One anonymous critic put up a wall poster at Qinghua University on June 2, 1957. "We have given our blood, sweat, toil and precious lives to defend not the people but the bureaucratic organs and bureaucrats who oppress the people and live off the fat of the land," the poster read. "They are a group of fascists who employ foul means, twist the truth, band together in evil adventure, and ignore the people's wish for peace." The diatribe went on to indict Mao as one "who enjoys the best things of life while the people suffer. . . . That son of a bitch! A million shames on him!"[16]

According to historians Gregor Benson and Alan Hunter,

> The bitter and sometimes inflammatory outpourings of the five weeks of freedom stunned [Mao] into recognizing the limits of his authority. Clearly he had been wrong to think that class struggle was at an end and that free debate would automatically produce "correct" ideas: for though the economy was socialist, old attitudes lived in the minds of the "bourgeois," as their "wild attacks" and anarchic behavior showed. The solution would have to be a return to "class dictatorship."[17]

Mao declared the flowers to be "poisonous weeds" and launched the Anti-Rightist Campaign to purge those who dared to speak out against Mao's version of communism. Deng Xiaoping (1904–1997), later supreme leader of China after Mao's death, conducted the campaign against the intellectuals. More than five hundred thousand persons were sent into exile in the countryside or to prison. Countless others were executed.

Jonathan Spence disagrees with the claim that Mao was trying to flush out his enemies in the Hundred Flowers Campaign. "It was, rather, a muddled and inconclusive movement that grew out of conflicting attitudes within the CCP leadership. At its center was an argument about the pace and type of development that was best for China."[18] The CCP leaders agreed that the agricultural sector would have to improve its yields to support development. How to accomplish that was the heart of the debate.

THE GREAT LEAP FORWARD

In 1958 Mao announced the launching of a bold new economic plan to increase China's industrial and agricultural outputs. He called the plan the Great Leap Forward. Mao urged the APCs to begin collectivization again, arguing that they had not really been given a chance. Many in the party bureaucracy resisted Mao's ideas and advocated instead centralized economic planning. They believed that Mao was going too fast in his collectivization policies.

Push came to shove within party ranks at a conference in Lushan. Only army marshal Peng Dehuai (1898–1974) was willing to criticize Mao's extremist economic policies. He sent a private letter to Mao. Mao responded in public to Peng by threatening to form a new Red Army and start a new revolution if he did not get his way. The party leadership removed Peng from his post. With all the party officials thoroughly intimidated, the Great Leap Forward proceeded as scheduled.

Several factors caused the agricultural collapse and famine that followed. Many peasants could not tend their fields because they had been ordered to work in industry or in massive irrigation and construction projects. Weather did not cooperate. Local officials vastly overreported grain yields because they feared being labeled counterrevolutionaries if they reported low yields. Peasants were harassed and punished for hoarding despite the fact that there was no grain to hoard. Adding to the peasants' problem was rampant corruption among local party cadres who stole from the peasants.

The biggest single factor that contributed to famine was forcing the peasants to eat at communal dining halls instead of at home. Up to that time, peasant families stored and carefully apportioned food to last through months of lean times until the next harvest. With the opening of the communal halls, peasants were told that they could eat as much as they wanted. Individual stores were banned. The waste and misuse of communal food stores was tremendous, and within a very short time, the food ran out.

The peasants much preferred to eat at home with their families, and to work their own plots of land, but this was not allowed during the Great Leap Forward. Mao complained later that the Chinese peasants had a "spontaneous desire to become capitalists"[19] because of their consistent desire to own their own land and improve their families' economic welfare.

The Great Leap Forward was a colossal failure. China entered into a bitter three years of severe famine (1959–1961).

In some provinces, entire villages disappeared because all the people had starved to death or moved away for lack of food. In others, peasants ate tree bark, grass, and even human corpses just to survive. Over the whole country, conservative estimates indicate that over 30 million people died. The famine following the Great Leap Forward is thought to be the worse single disaster in human history, and undoubtedly it was Mao's greatest failure. Although there were early and consistent reports of famine, Mao chose to believe those lower officials who were too afraid to give him anything other than positive reports. Finally, when the starvation reports became too persistent to ignore, Mao called out the PLA and began distributing grain to the beleaguered peasants.

Good relations with the Soviet Union had declined at the same time as the Great Leap Forward. The new leader in Moscow, Nikita Khrushchev (1894–1971) was grudging in his support of the Chinese. By 1960 the Soviets had removed all their technical advisers from China.

Mao lost considerable authority when it became clear that his economic policies were a disaster. Party bureaucrats reversed the collectivization trend, and economic recovery began immediately. For the first time, Mao Zedong Thought came into question. Even in moral authority, Mao lost ground. He had isolated himself from the common people and lived like a modern-day emperor attended by servants in luxurious surroundings. Estranged from his wife, Jiang Qing, Mao became notorious for his brief sexual liaisons with young peasant girls. Straitlaced Li Zhisui, Mao's physician, was appalled at Mao's claim that his sexual activity was a Daoist practice certain to enhance his longevity.

Sidelined from party politics, Mao plotted his return to power. He had several allies to aid his cause. One was Lin Biao (1908–1971), a wartime military leader who now began resurrecting the latent cult of Mao that had existed since Yanan days. Lin Biao published a book of Mao's quotations and distributed it to PLA members. The book, wrapped in red plastic, became known throughout the world as the Little Red Book. It proved to be a much-studied guide for revolutionaries during the trying times ahead. Another Mao ally was his wife, Jiang Qing, who began to concern herself with what she saw as the "feudal" nature of much of China's art. Art and culture were important to Mao because of his interest in thought reform through education. Mao's old hatchet man from Yanan days, Kang Sheng, joined these two to work for Mao's return to power.

By 1966 Chinese Communist Party officials were dividing into two camps. One camp was made up of professional party bureaucrats and intellectuals who were interested in a planned economy and an effective governmental bureaucracy. The other was a radical leftist faction identified with Mao and led by Jiang Qing, which wanted to continue the revolutionary class struggle and collectivization. Lines were being drawn for the great ideological struggle to come.

THE CULTURAL REVOLUTION

The Cultural Revolution began in 1966 when a radical leftist philosophy professor at Beijing University, Nie Yuanzi, hung a poster criticizing university administrators who were aligned with the party bureaucracy. Everyone waited breathlessly to see if she would be purged or praised for her audacity. Meanwhile, groups of students who called themselves Red Guards initiated protests and other disturbances on university campuses. Mao praised both Nie's poster and the revolutionary spirit of the Red Guards, and the Cultural Revolution was launched.

Given this green light from Mao, youthful Red Guard gangs (most were middle-school students and numbered in the millions) began attacking the "four olds": old ideas, old culture, old customs, and old habits. Their intent was to identify and destroy any remnants of feudalism or reactionary thinking in Chinese society. Confucian temples and shrines, libraries, and schools were looted, and thousands of books were burned. Property was vandalized or destroyed. Teachers, parents, and officials were called out, beaten, humiliated, and forced to perform menial tasks. Anyone associated with anything labeled *rightist* was persecuted. Thousands of intellectuals lost their jobs. Thousands of party officials were accused of being rightists and were purged. Many intellectuals were jailed and executed. Schools were shut down in the cities, and a generation of university students was forced to leave school. Individuals were classified by "revolutionary" bloodlines, and trouble came upon those with capitalist or rightist ancestors. The violence of the Cultural Revolution was uncoordinated, uncontrolled, pervasive, and terrifying. Even Mao was surprised by the excesses of the Red Guard.

Accompanying the Red Guards' violence was an unquestioning allegiance to Mao. The cult of Mao reached excessive extremes during the Cultural Revolution. Mao's picture was posted everywhere. Everyone wore Mao badges and diligently studied the Little Red Book. He was venerated as if he were a semireligious figure or an emperor.

Jiang Qing, Mao's wife from Yanan days, was put in charge of cultural affairs, an important position because Mao had long seen art, literature, film, and philosophy as a place where ideological purity must be maintained. Jiang Qing and three comrades formed what came to be called the Gang of Four. During the Cultural Revolution, Jiang and her gang arranged for purges of party members who, in the gang's eyes, were not sufficiently revolutionary. Jiang Qing plotted and schemed to position herself to take over the government after Mao's death. Mao complained about her meddling in political affairs, but he refused to purge her. Jiang Qing was arrested after Mao's death for crimes committed during the Cultural Revolution. She claimed in her trial that she had only been obeying Mao's orders. When she was found guilty and her sentence was handed down, she shouted to the judge that it was no crime to make a revolution. Defiant to the end, Jiang Qing committed suicide in prison in 1991. Her last words condemned her enemies, among them Deng Xiaoping, as revisionists who had abandoned Mao's Communist revolution.

Anarchy reigned during the height of the Cultural Revolution, and Mao lost control of the leftist extremists. When Red Guard factions began to fight among themselves, the PLA had to be called out to control them. Civil war looked eminent, and Mao realized that things had gone too far. He began to reign in the youthful Red Guard by sending them in small groups to the countryside to learn from the peasants. The worst violence of the Cultural Revolution was over by 1969, but the purges and the terror lingered on for years.

A REASSESSMENT OF THE CULTURAL REVOLUTION

The Cultural Revolution has been described by many Chinese people as "ten years of madness." Scholars have documented the violence accompanying the Red Guards' revolutionary zeal, and the suffering that resulted. However, there are historians who have began to reassess the Cultural Revolution and to suggest that some good actually came from it.

Without denying the horrific violence that occurred, historian Lee Feigon lauds Mao for two positive accomplishments coming from the upheaval. First was the impact of Mao's policies on China's economic development and political reform. "Not only did Mao begin the process of opening up China to the outside world [Mao invited U.S. president Richard Nixon to China in 1972], he also created the industrial infrastructure that laid the basis for the resuscitation of the Chinese economy during the Deng years."[20]

In addition, Mao attacked and reduced the size and power of the entrenched Communist Party bureaucracy during the Cultural Revolution. Mao believed that the party and the government had become corrupt and authoritarian. Mao said, "At present you can buy a branch secretary for a few packs of cigarettes, not to mention marrying a daughter to him."[21] He had always been suspicious of bureaucracies. Now it was his own bureaucracy that Mao attacked. As Feigon writes, "Not only did [Mao] succeed in ousting more than 70 percent of the Chinese Communist Party's Central Committee, he also reduced and decentralized the Soviet-style bureaucracy that was threatening to choke China, pruning it to one-sixth its former size. The impact of this bureaucratic cleanup was far-reaching, with especially salubrious [healthful] effects on China's economy."[22]

Feigon points out that Mao's long-standing concern for the Chinese peasant held steady during the Cultural Revolution. Advances in health care and education directly benefited the 85 percent of China's population that lived in rural areas. For example, country medical workers, called "barefoot doctors," received training in China's cities and then returned to their native villages to provide medical care to the peasants.

Although many urban schools were closed, education dramatically expanded to peasant communities in the years 1966 to 1976. Feigon asserts, "The Cultural Revolution is usually thought of as a period in which Mao closed the schools and ended all learning. In fact it was a time when the number of schools increased exponentially and learning was extended to huge areas of previously neglected parts of the country."[23] The number of people attending middle schools grew by 700 percent during the Cultural Revolution. Mao continued to demonstrate his lifelong interest in providing education to the poor rural peasant.

THE LAST YEARS

Mao's last years were dominated by a struggle against ill health and approaching death. By 1974 Mao was so affected by Parkinson's disease and other disorders that he could no longer speak. Yet he clung to power. The year 1976 was significant in China. On July 28, a massive earthquake shook the Hebei province. The city of Tangshan was destroyed, and 242,000 of its residents were killed. Many Chinese saw the earthquake as a portent. Then, on September 11, Mao died.

For a short time, a power struggle ensued, then a new leader emerged, Deng Xiaoping. During the Cultural Revolution, Deng had been accused by Mao of being a "capitalist roader," and he had been purged. Perhaps the accusations were true because when he took power, Deng immediately set China on the road to such dramatic economic changes that China is now described by scholars as a capitalist, not Communist, economy. New classes have appeared in Chinese society, and the revolution as Mao defined it no longer exists. Despite this, Deng and Mao shared one common vision. They both believed that the Chinese Communist Party should rule China, and it continues to do so today.

Mao's efforts to provide education for the Chinese peasants have been undermined. Historian Feigon says, "Since Mao's death, his successors have gutted the rural educational system he put in place—once again discriminating against people from poor rural backgrounds. This despite the fact that almost everywhere resources devoted to rural education remain the most efficient way to promote economic development."[24]

Jasper Becker, who also has written about contemporary Chinese education, points out that parents must pay tuition now, even for primary school, whereas it had been free during the Cultural Revolution. Most of the state funding for Chinese education goes to "key" schools that serve only a small number of students. Private fee-paying schools have appeared recently to serve the new rich. These schools are called "aristocracy schools."[25]

Historians continue to evaluate the role of Mao in Chinese history. Some see him as China's most important ruler since the first emperor, Qin Shihuangdi. Others say that the reformers who came after Mao, not Mao himself, will have a greater impact on China in the long run. Questions remain about Mao's motivations. Was he a man of the people who consistently acted on behalf of China's poor rural peasants? Or was he a power-mad tyrant devoted only to maintaining his power? More likely, he was some of both. He served the people, then lost touch with them. In the end, he lived out his days not as a idealized peasant but as an emperor.

NOTES

1. Dick Wilson, *Mao: The People's Emperor.* London: Hutchinson, 1979, p. 447.

2. Lee Feigon, *Mao: A Reinterpretation.* Chicago: Ivan R. Dee, 2002, p. 16.

3. Quoted in Edgar Snow, *Red Star over China.* New York: Random House, 1968, p. 135.

4. Quoted in Snow, *Red Star over China,* p. 151.

5. Feigon, *Mao,* p. 38.

6. Quoted in Philip Short, *Mao: A Life.* London: Hodder & Stoughton, 1999, p. 203.

7. Short, *Mao,* p. 226.

8. Jonathan D. Spence, *Mao Zedong.* New York: Penguin Putnam, 1999, pp. 82–83.

9. John King Fairbank, *China: A New History.* Cambridge, MA: Harvard University Press, 1992, pp. 317–19.

10. Edward J. Lazzerini, *The Chinese Revolution.* Westport, CT: Greenwood Press, 1999, p. 44.

11. Lazzerini, *The Chinese Revolution,* p. 45.

12. Spence, *Mao Zedong,* p. 93.

13. Quoted in Ross Terrill, *Mao: A Biography.* Stanford, CA: Stanford University Press, 1999, p. 226.

14. J.A.G. Roberts, *Modern China: An Illustrated History.* Gloucestershire, UK: Sutton, 1998, p. 221.

15. Quoted in Jonathan D. Spence, *The Search for Modern China.* New York: W.W. Norton, 1990, p. 568.

16. Anonymous, "I Accuse, I Protest," June 2, 1957, in *Wild Lily, Prairie Fire: China's Road to Democracy, Yan'an to Tian'anmen, 1942–1989,* ed. Gregor Benton and Alan Hunter. Princeton, NJ: Princeton University Press, 1995, p. 100.

17. Benson and Hunter, *Wild Lily, Prairie Fire,* p. 16.

18. Spence, *The Search for Modern China,* p. 574.

19. Quoted in Edgar Snow, *The Long Revolution.* New York: Random House, 1972, p. 61.

20. Feigon, *Mao,* p. 8.

21. Mao Zedong, "Talk on Questions of Philosophy," in *Chairman*

Mao Talks to the People, Talks and Letters, 1956–1971, ed. Stuart Schram. New York: Pantheon Books, p. 217.

22. Feigon, *Mao,* pp. 139–40.
23. Feigon, *Mao,* p. 142.
24. Feigon, Mao, p. 143.
25. Jasper Becker, *The Chinese.* New York: Free Press, 2000, p. 217.

A NOTE ABOUT CHINESE PINYIN LANGUAGE

Chinese written language is readable to Chinese people everywhere regardless of the dialect spoken. However, Chinese characters make little sense to Westerners unless they are trained to read them. Systems of transliterating these characters—that is, changing into a different alphabet—have been developed to make it possible for Westerners to read Chinese.

There are two systems of transliteration. The Wade-Giles system was used for many years, and this system is still found in older books. The pinyin system was officially adopted by the Chinese government in the 1950s and is used everywhere today in China. When pinyin was established, names such as *Peking* under the Wade-Giles system became *Beijing*. *Mao Tse-tung* became *Mao Zedong*.

For Westerners, there are two important pronunciation keys: The pinyin *q* is pronounced "ch," and *x* is pronounced as "sh." Therefore, *Qing* is pronounced "Ching," and *Xia* is pronounced "Shia" or "shi-ah."

This book generally uses the pinyin system. However, if an article was written using the Wade-Giles system, that system is retained, and pinyin names are included in parentheses. Exceptions to this are names that are very well known under the Wade-Giles system, such as *Chiang Kai-shek* and *Sun Yat-sen*.

Regarding Chinese names, the surname (family name) is given first and the personal name follows. For example, Mao is Mao Zedong's surname.

CHAPTER 1

FROM PEASANT WORKER TO COMMUNIST ORGANIZER

PEOPLE
WHO MADE
HISTORY

MAO ZEDONG

Mao's Youth

Jeffrey G. Barlow

Mao Zedong was born during a time of political and
social upheaval in China. Despite the uncertain
times, Mao's childhood in rural Hunan province was
quiet. He was born into a prosperous peasant family
and began working in the fields early in life. Jeffrey
G. Barlow, professor of history at Pacific University,
explains that Mao rebelled against both his domi-
neering father and his teachers. The young Mao preferred reading romantic adventure tales instead of
the required Confucian classics. Despite his early
propensity to rebel, Mao became interested in fur-
thering his education and eventually graduated from
a teacher's college. He was drawn to reformist and
revolutionary political ideas and eventually joined
the Chinese Communist Party. Barlow is the author
of several books and articles on Chinese history, including *Sun Yat-sen and the French, 1900–1908.*

Mao Zedong was born into a China weakened by overpopu-
lation and economic decline and faced with an inability to
halt the aggressive and expanding Western nations in the
mid-19th century. While the ostensible causes of conflict
were China's refusal to trade with the West, the struggle was
really a collision of the traditional Chinese system and the
modernizing West. After the British defeated China in a series of clashes called the Opium Wars (1839–42), the country was opened to foreign trade and influences with which
it was ill-prepared to cope. The Taiping Rebellion (1850–64),
an immense civil war, began in this confusion. As many as
40 million Chinese may have died, including millions in Hunan [province], where Mao would be born in the aftermath
of this chaos in 1893.

The traditional Chinese political system was a monarchy
headed by hereditary emperors. Each era dominated by a

particular family was entitled a "dynasty." When Mao was born, the last dynasty, the Manchu-Qing (Ch'ing), was tottering to its close. But as the Chinese say, "Heaven is high, and the Emperor far away." Where Mao lived, in the small village of Shaoshan in Hunan province in central China below the Yangtze river, people were comparatively isolated.

Mao's father Mao Jen-shen (1870–1920) had been a poor peasant and briefly a soldier. He married an older woman, Wen Qimei (Wen Ch'i-mei) (d. 1918), who gave birth first to Mao; then in 1898, to a second brother, Mao Zemin; and in 1905 to a third, Mao Zetan. In that same year, the family also adopted a daughter, Mao Zehung.

MAO'S YOUTH

In some respects, Mao's childhood was an idyllic one. Unusually tall for his age, he had a strong constitution and an intense manner. The family was increasingly well-off and never lacked, as many Chinese families did, for enough to eat or adequate clothing. The surrounding countryside was a series of beautiful low hills and lovely rice paddies. In one of Mao's many poems, "Return to Shaoshan," translated by Jerome Ch'en and Michael Bullock, he later eulogized the area, saying, "In delight I watched a thousand waves of growing rice."

But Mao's father, deeply marked by his years struggling to survive in rural China and doubtlessly carrying many memories of the starvation and suffering of the Taiping years, ruled the family with an iron hand. He was cruel to family members and hired help alike. Mao and his mother were forced close together by their suffering at his father's hands, and it may be that Mao's unusual sensitivity to the problems of Chinese women, who were greatly oppressed by feudal society, began at this time.

Some scholars have argued that it was Mao Zedong's continual conflicts with his father that set him off on a life of revolution. Whatever the cause, the young Mao seems to have been a rebel from the beginning, rebelling against the constraints of the very hierarchical traditional Chinese family, and particularly, against the foreign domination of his country.

Put to work in the fields at the age of five, Mao had to wait until he was seven, somewhat old for boys in his age group, before he could start school. He read the required works of history and great literature, but he also loved the colorful traditional Chinese novels, like *The Water Margin* and *The Romance of the Three Kingdoms*, both lengthy tales of rebels and heroes which have sometimes been compared to the Robin Hood stories. Later, as a rebel at the head of peasant bands, Mao was able to draw on those novels for lessons to be applied in the desperate struggles of guerilla war.

In 1908, Mao's father, in the traditional fashion, tried to arrange a marriage for his son, perhaps to keep him at home and discourage his modern ideas of pursuing an education. Mao refused to recognize the marriage and claimed never to have had a relationship with this local girl, the first of his four wives.

In 1910, Mao was sent to a more modern school in a nearby town, where classmates were mostly sons of wealthier families, and where the rawboned Mao, already hardened by physical labor, was first turned away from the gate on his arrival. But Mao's superior abilities gained him the respect of teachers and classmates alike. He read widely, devouring both the traditional learning and the works of reformers who advocated more modern responses to China's acute problems. In 1911, his abilities took him to the provincial capital, Changsha, and to middle school, where he wished to continue his study. Had China been a stable country, it is probable that Mao would have finished out his life as a scholar. In his old age, he said that he wished to be remembered, above all, as a teacher.

MAO'S INTEREST IN REVOLUTION

But during Mao's youth, China was collapsing. The Manchu-Qing dynasty which had conquered China in the 17th century fell apart in 1911. Chinese were briefly optimistic while revolutionaries led by Sun Yat-sen (1866–1925) seemed to offer hope for a new China. Mao himself was so moved by the promise of revolution that he walked for days to Wuhan, where Sun's Republican forces were taking the city from Manchu troops. Here Mao saw his first sizeable city, and his first battle with its inevitable streets full of corpses. He served for some time in the Republican ranks, though he did not fight.

But Sun Yat-sen proved unable to consolidate a unified government, and by 1916, China was in the grip of military men, the "Warlords." Some of these men were true patriots who ruled skillfully and wisely, others were brutal adventurers who taxed and pillaged the peasants beyond endurance.

From 1913 to 1918, Mao studied at the provincial teacher's training college in Changsha. There he read widely in Western works, and in the radical Chinese writings of the "New

CONFUCIANISM IN MAO'S LIFE

Like most Chinese children born in the nineteenth century who had access to education, Mao was trained in the Confucian classics. Intellectuals of the May 4 and New Culture movements, and Mao, too, would reject Confucianism as "feudal." Mao biographer Philip Short points out that as he grew older, Mao again turned to the old master for inspiration and guidance.

For Mao, as for all Chinese of his generation, the importance of [Confucian] texts and their commentaries, together with the Four Books—the Confucian *Analects*, the *Great Learning*, the *Doctrine of the Mean* and the works of Mencius—which he studied next, cannot be overstated. The ideas they contained, the way those ideas were formulated and the values and concepts that underpinned them, fixed the underlying pattern of Mao's thought for the rest of his life, just as surely as, in Western countries, the parameters of thought for atheists, no less than believers, are defined by Judæo-Christian values and ideas. . . .

More broadly, Mao drew from Confucianism three key ideas which were to prove fundamental to the whole of his later thought. These were, first, the notion that every human being, and every society, must have a moral compass; if not Confucianism, then something else which fulfils that role. The second was the primacy of right-thinking, which Confucius called 'virtue': only if a person's thoughts were right—not merely correct, but morally right—would his actions be right. Third was the importance of self-cultivation.

Mao claimed to dislike the Classics, but his fondness for quoting them belies that. His speeches in later life were packed with allusions to Confucius, to the Daoist thinker, Zhuangzi, to the Mohists and other early philosophical schools, far outnumbering those to Lenin and Marx. Theirs were the ideas with which he grew up, and which he knew better than any other. The Confucian legacy would prove at least as important to him as Marxism, and in the last years of his life it became once more ascendant.

Philip Short, *Mao: A Life.* New York: Henry Holt & Company, 1999.

Culture Movement" which was then sweeping China. Throwing himself into the political life of the day, Mao formed student groups, founded a special school to teach workers to read, edited literary and political magazines, demonstrated against the warlord governor of the province, protested school rules which hampered student political activity, and published an article in *New Youth,* the central journal of the nationwide protest movement. He somehow also found time to fall in love with Yang K'ai-hui (1901–1930), the daughter of a favorite professor, and in 1920, married her. She bore him a son.

While student radicals and intellectuals like Mao were interested in Western learning, they were also exceptionally critical of Western thought which seemed to often be contradicted by Western actions which tore at China's vitals. The warlords depended to a large degree on Western sources of arms and munitions, and Western countries competed eagerly to make extortionate loans and unequal treaties which eroded Chinese sovereignty. Chinese reformers like Sun Yat-sen could not gain international support for unifying China, because foreign governments rightly suspected that any real Chinese government would be aggressively nationalist and would attempt to rectify foreign domination of a divided China.

THE APPEAL OF MARXISM AND COMMUNISM

For Chinese reformers, the Russian Bolshevik Revolution in 1918 was an intoxicating event. Led by [Vladimir] Lenin (1870–1924), the Bolsheviks destroyed the tsarist autocracy and established a revolutionary government. Chinese were drawn to the Russian example because there were many superficial similarities between the two countries. Both were traditional monarchies, both were largely backward and agrarian, and, to the Chinese, Russia was as much Asian as European. Chinese interest in the Russian revolution soon led them to Lenin and to Karl Marx [Political Theorist, 1818–1883].

The Russian revolutionaries were equally interested in China. Fearing that the Western powers, especially Great Britain, were determined to stifle their infant revolution, the Russians eagerly sought allies. It was obvious to them that China was on the verge of some titanic upheaval which, with proper assistance, might become a second Communist revolution. The Russians sent political advisors to the radical Chinese groups.

From earnest circles of students reading Marxist literature, like one in which Mao himself was engaged, small Communist groups began to emerge. In 1921, when some of these men met in Shanghai—the great Chinese city at the mouth of the Yangtze river—to found the Chinese Communist party, Mao was one of them.

Although Mao was soon a convinced Marxist, he was always clear that for him Marxism was not an end in itself, and certainly not a doctrine that would ever lead him to subordinate China to Russia, but an instrument with which to free China. As Mao said, "Marxism is the arrow with which we will hit the target of the Chinese revolution."

But for young Chinese Communists, life in the 1920s was very complex. As the Russians looked about China, they found their interests drawn not to the nascent Chinese Communist party, but to a far larger and better organized group, the Nationalist party (Kuomintang; often known as the KMT), begun by Sun Yat-sen. As a frustrated Chinese Nationalist, Sun Yat-sen welcomed help from any quarter. With Soviet assistance, he built a military organization and modern party along Soviet lines, then prepared for a march north from his base in the south at Canton to defeat the warlords and unify China.

The Communist party agreed to Soviet demands that they cooperate with the KMT. The young Communists threw their energies into helping prepare the way for the march north. Mao, because of his charisma, his experience, and his peasant background, soon became the group's primary activist among Chinese peasants. But as Mao studied peasant suffering and recalled his life as a child in the countryside, he began to make an important break with orthodox Marxist doctrines.

MAO AND CHINA'S PEASANTS

According to Marx and Lenin, the heart of any revolutionary Communist movement had to be urban workers or the proletariat. Mao observed that the peasants were not only far more numerous than China's minuscule proletariat, but were themselves spontaneously rising from centuries of misery at the hands of rural landlords to create their own revolutions. As Mao said in his report on an "Investigation of the Peasant Movement in Hunan" in March of 1927:

> The present upsurge of the peasant movement is a colossal event. In a very short time, in China's central, southern and northern provinces, several hundred million peasants will rise like a mighty storm, like a hurricane, a force so swift and violent that no power, however great, will be able to hold it back.

This was the key realization of Mao's life, and from it came his central strategy: the peasants would be the backbone of the Chinese revolution. Whoever gave them proper leadership and genuinely served their interests would lead China.

The May Fourth Movement and Mao

Ross Terrill

China was in political chaos in the years after the death of President Yuan Shikai in 1916. Warlords took control and ruled their territory with iron hands. Yet the next decade also would be one of great intellectual ferment in China. Scholars have called it China's Renaissance. The May Fourth Movement (May 4, 1919) was a patriotic movement that erupted when the Japanese were allowed to control China's Shandong Province in accordance with the Treaty of Versailles that ended World War I.

Associated with the May Fourth Movement was an explosion of intellectual activity that is sometimes called the New Culture Movement. This movement, centered in Beijing, rejected traditional Confucian values as "feudal." New ideas from the West such as democracy, Marxism, feminism, and scientific empiricism were enthusiastically considered. Calls were made to adopt the common, everyday Chinese language instead of the old classical style. Anti-imperialism and a strong Chinese nationalism developed from the May Fourth Movement. Founders of the new Chinese Communist Party, such as Chen Duxiu (1879–1942) and Li Dazhao (1888–1927) were both leaders in the New Culture Movement.

Mao was heavily influenced by the patriotic fervor and the influx of new ideas when he traveled to Beijing in 1918. Ross Terrill, a research scholar at Harvard University, relates that in these heady times, Mao first adopted anarchism, then turned to Marxism as his guiding political philosophy. In his early political writings, Mao balked at foreign occupation and the oppressive policies of feudal rulers in China. Instead of advocating a revision of the political system, he seized on the notion that China would require a whole new society.

Ross Terrill, *Mao: A Biography.* Stanford, CA: Stanford University Press, 1999. Copyright © 1999 by Ross Terrill. All rights reserved. Reproduced by permission.

The Chinese Revolution began in a library. A doctrine was needed to give direction to the formless revolt against the old. One had long existed—since Karl Marx sat in another, British library, when Mao's grandfather was a boy. Bits of it had even been translated into Chinese not long before World War I. But only with the Bolshevik Revolution did the doctrine come alive for Chinese minds.

Marxism was one thing; an interesting theory with a message mainly for the advanced countries. Leninism was not the same. If backward Russia could make a Marxist revolution, and if imperialism by its own logic was going to provoke socialism (as Lenin said it would), might not China be part of the action? Maybe those difficult essays by Marx were worth a more careful look? So after 1917 a few keen Chinese hunted down Marxist articles and pamphlets in Mao's library.

Mao could read to his fill without buying so much as a daily paper—a boon for his pitiful budget—and for the first time he read Marx and Lenin.

Yet Mao failed to get hold of Marxism that winter. The idea that bubbled highest in the cauldron of his mind was anarchism. He read more Kropotkin than Marx. He understood the passionate Russian more readily than the systematic German.

Like any anarchist, Mao knew better what he was against than what he was for. As yet he had no intellectual weapon to attack militarism and imperialism with. In personal terms too, anarchism was a fit doctrine for the unconnected existence Mao led that winter.

THE MOVEMENT BEGINS

In the spring of 1919, Peking erupted in a student demonstration—to be called the May Fourth Movement—that brought to a peak all the themes of *New Youth*. But Mao was out of step. He was in one of his clouded moods, when resolve did not quite surface. He turned in upon himself at the very moment when a public cause gripped the Peking student body. He left Peking, alone, and for an unexpected destination.

As the students tore strips off Confucianism, Mao went to visit Confucius's grave in Shandong Province.

"I saw the small stream where Confucius's disciples bathed their feet," he related, "and the little town where the sage lived as a child." He climbed sacred Mount Tai. He inspected the birthplace of Mencius. The tour took him through territory—Liang Shan county—where his heroes of the novel *Story of the Marshes* had performed their exploits.

As the radicals in Peking declared the Old a heap of refuse. Mao indulged himself at founts of the Old. On May Fourth the first mass movement of intellectuals in Chinese history took shape, to burn tradition and to defy Japan's arrogance toward China. But Mao was in touch only with the hills and walls of China. . . .

He went to see his second "model" from the pages of *New Youth*, Professor Chen Duxiu, a literature scholar from Peking who had moved to Shanghai in 1917 under the whip of warlord repression [Mao's first "model" was Peking University librarian Li Dazhao]. A seed was planted for future contact, yet this first meeting set neither man on fire.

Mao walked the streets, read newspapers, looked up Hunanese friends.

His mind was straying back to events in Changsha. It came as good news when the group organizing work-study in France gave him money to go back to Hunan. Mao wrapped up his books, clothes, and documents and in April 1919 made the complicated foot-train-steamer journey to Changsha. . . .

It turned out that the north had left its mark on him. Silent in Peking, he now had a lot to say in Changsha. His first venture was a public lecture on the newfangled idea called *Makesi zhuyi* (Marxism), which he knew a bit about but only a bit.

MAO PROMOTES MAY FOURTH IDEALS

During the second half of 1919 Mao became a spearhead for New Culture and anti-imperialism—May Fourth's twin themes—in the Changsha area. Chief target was the warlord ruler of Hunan, Zhang Jingyao, a caricature of the half-feudal, pro-Japan fudger that made May Fourth students see red.

Mao took the lead in the Changsha wing of May Fourth with two well-run undertakings. As the sun baked Changsha in June, he helped bring to birth a United Students' Association of Hunan.

The social atmosphere of this student movement has never been quite matched for ardor; not in China, nor in the U.S. during the 1960s. Schools were closed half the time (ideological "truth" pushed out factual truth). All night long, manifestoes were drawn up for yet one more demonstration the next day. Toothbrushes in pockets, carrying umbrellas with towels wrapped around them, students fanned out from Changsha to link up with the like-minded elsewhere. Nearly everyone was in a state of war with his or her family. Crudely printed little magazines appeared, with titles that conveyed the mood of uplift: *Awakening, Women's Bell, New Culture, Warm Tide, Upward, Strife, New Voice.* . . .

A student cut off two fingers as his personal protest against Governor Zhang's brutal methods. Thirteen-year-old Ding Ling, later to be one of China's best short-story writers, led her class to the chambers of the Hunan Provincial Council to demand for women the equal right to inherit property. The younger they were, the fewer doubts they had.

Mao spoke to a rally on the theme "Use National Products: Resist Japanese Goods," not facing the fact that Chinese products were inadequate to the people's needs. He organized teams of girls—from the start he brought women into the heart of the United Students' Association of Hunan—to inspect Changsha shops and browbeat the owners into destroying Japanese imports.

Mao later recalled that "No one had time for love." It was true that women and men slept chastely side by side. An hour or two's repose after a night of political busyness did not lend itself to caresses. Mao, "three heroes" member Cai Hesen, and his bright and pretty sister Cai Chang, swore a triangular oath to marry. All three broke it and Mao broke it three times. . . .

MAO'S MAGAZINE

During this stormy summer Mao, acting for the students' association, founded, edited, and wrote large portions of a weekly which he characteristically named after nature: *Xiang River Review.* Two thousand copies of the *Review's* first issue were sold in a single day and five thousand copies of subsequent issues were printed (a big print run for Hunan in 1919).

The magazine set its type where its mouth was. Expressing a cultural aim of May Fourth, it used "plain talk" (*baihua*), the language much as it is spoken, rather than the rigid archaic form (*wenyan*). The change was like replacing the language of the King James version of the Bible with that of *Jesus Christ Superstar.*

It was true, as even Professor Hu Shi said, that Mao was an arresting writer. His paragraphs, drafted on thin, red-ruled paper, were blunt and vivid. His avid newspaper reading bore fruit in detailed illustrations for each point.

"The movement for the liberation of mankind has shot forward," editor Mao declared in his inaugural piece. "What are the things which we should not be afraid of?" He gave an answer that showed the supermarket nature of his mind at that time: "We should not be afraid of Heaven, of gods, of ghosts, of the dead, or of warlords and capitalists." . . .

Mao wrote an article called "Great Union of the Popular Masses," which summed up his views. It was eloquent, populist, and patriotic. Not a bit Marxist, it was nevertheless sharply different from his "Study of Physical Culture" of two years before.

Mao began with a dire diagnosis: "The decadence of the state, the sufferings of humanity, and the darkness of society have all reached an extreme." He no longer saw steeled individuals as the solution. Such self-cultivated monks—first among them Mao Zedong—would be needed to initiate China's climb out of darkness. But Mao did not broach leadership in "Great Union of the Popular Masses."

He rabble-roused for the widest possible support. He called people from all strata to join hands and "shout" against oppression. The union was to be part mystical and part organizational. Solidarity was the key. The 1911 revolution had not involved the ordinary people—the next one must.

Marx was mentioned ("the German, Marx") in order to be compared unfavorably to Mao's favorite anarchist ("the Russian, Kropotkin"). Mao said the standpoint of Marx was extremely violent." The more moderate standpoint of Kropotkin might not yield overnight results. But its supreme virtue was that it "begins by understanding the common people."

The piece was revolutionary, but in the Changsha of 1919 Marx seemed no more logical as theorist in chief of revolution than a half-dozen others. Mao had a vision of a more-just social order. He had a sharp organizational instinct. But he did not yet have an ideology. . . .

In starting to publish his views Mao crossed a threshold. One thing to read and study and write ten thousand words of notes in the margins of a textbook. Quite a fresh thing to take a stand in public. This was action, it was confession, it had consequences. Mao was no longer merely exploring the world around him, but taking steps to shape it.

It was one of warlord Zhang's habits to extinguish left-wing magazines as a janitor turns out lights during an energy crisis. An armed detachment arrived one midnight at the Graceful Xiang Printing Company. The *Review* was dead after five issues and its parent, the United Students' Association of Hunan, was stamped out the same night.

Small magazines were then like birds that flew by and were gone. Mao soon joined himself to the flight of another one, *New Hunan*. Run by medical students . . . , equally a voice of May Fourth, it was short of help during the summer months and welcomed Mao as editor. Begun in June, taken over by Mao in August, it died the same death as the *Review* in October—but not before attracting some more favorable leftist national attention for Mao's pen.

THE CASE OF MISS ZHAO

He was well enough launched now as a political writer that his pieces were taken by *Great Welfare Daily*, the leading Changsha paper. Suddenly there was a fresh cause to write about.

A Miss Zhao of Changsha was to be married. She did not like the man chosen for her. But all four parents—her father was a spectacle-maker, the young man's father ran a curio shop—insisted on their carefully arranged match. The wedding day came. Dressed in her finery, Miss Zhao was borne aloft in a bridal sedan chair. The stiff parade marched off toward the groom's home. In a flash, Miss Zhao pulled out a razor from under her petticoats and slit her throat.

Within two days of the tragedy, Mao was in print with "A Critique of Miss Zhao's Suicide." Eight more articles by him on marriage, family oppression, and the evil of the old society peppered the columns of *Great Welfare Daily* over the next two weeks.

As so often, Mao dug from his own life the root of a social conviction.

He blamed society. "The circumstances of an event provide all the causes of its occurrence." Even in translation his prose thumps down: "The circumstances were the rotten marriage system, the benighted social system, thought which cannot be independent, love which cannot be free." He called Zhao's bridal sedan chair a "prisoner's cart."

One sniffs between the lines of these nine articles Mao's own arranged marriage and his mother's meek submission to a man for whom the term "male chauvinism" would be the understatement of the Chinese Revolution.

Mao assumed a paternal air with his "Advice to Boys and Girls on the Marriage Problem." In another piece he begged his readers to "shout" and thus bring down the house of cards that is superstition. Boldness as its own reward was already one of his beliefs. "Everyone regards predestined marriage as a sort of 'beautiful destiny.' *No one has ever imagined that it is all a mistake.*"

He began his lifelong opposition to suicide in any situation. "If in the end one does not succeed, one's energies are wholly spent and one dies in battle like the lost jade, this after all is true courage and the sort of tragedy which satisfies most." To kill oneself as Miss Zhao had was not to oppose the corrupt old society. It was to affirm that doomed order, to fit in with it. Struggle, do not commit suicide, Mao laid down.

Mao swiped at shrines to female chastity, which were in those days thought impressive: "Where are the shrines for chaste boys?" asked the man who had dallied with a couple of village girls. Next, he had girls out in the street cajoling housewives to reject Japanese goods, and drumming up support for a strike to thwart warlord Zhang.

In Mao's mind the link went back to the name of his New People's Study Society. The women's movement was a bid for new people. But Mao was coming close to the viewpoint that a *new society* was the ultimate goal.

Mao and his friends were on a collision course with Zhang's Hunan regime and December 1919 brought the crunch. Zhang's troops used swords and rifle butts to disperse a crowd making a bonfire of Japanese goods at Education Square. Late-night planning meetings followed one after the other. Mao wrote a manifesto urging the overthrow of pro-Japan, feudal, butcher Zhang.

Thirteen thousand students and their allies signed Mao's document. A Changsha-wide strike began; the issue was joined. Zhang was not overthrown—though his regime was bruised—and the trail was hot for Mao and other leaders.

Mao decided to leave Hunan: to escape Zhang, who now felt a personal fury for him, and to seek support in anti-warlord circles outside Hunan for the anti-Zhang cause.

MISS YANG

Mao went back to Peking. Four months there were a time of harvest for him, though not in fully expected ways. . . .

Mao rented part of the old and crumbling Fuyu lamasery

on North Avenue by the moat of the Imperial Palace. He slept in the main hall of the unheated temple, under the eyes of gilded Tibetan gods. His desk for night reading and writing was an incense table made eerie by the glow of an oil lamp. A mimeograph machine—chalice of the new era of political organizing—stood by the incense table. It formed the plant for what the young provincial politician grandly called Common People's News Agency.

Mao did not achieve much for the anti-Zhang cause. Peking was a wider world in the grip of larger concerns: the downward spiral of a "national" government headed by a glorified warlord; global gyrations after Versailles; echoes of the Bolshevik Revolution; the playing out of May Fourth's themes. Mao knocked on many doors but often got a glazed look when he broached Hunan's affairs.

Mao's first Peking harvest was Miss Yang. Eight years younger than Mao, Yang Kaihui was a slight girl, with a round face and a pale complexion for a southern Chinese. Mao's affection for her had grown during his previous stay in Peking. Now things advanced a stage further.

Professor Yang died a month after Mao reached the capital, and the loss seemed to clear Mao's way to physical intimacy with Kaihui.

The life of the couple began as a "trial marriage," which Professor Yang might not have liked, but in Peking they did not set up house together. They met amid the statues in Mao's feudal chamber on North Avenue, or at the warmer and more comfortable Yang family home. When spring came they would go for a pony ride along the ridges of the Western Hills and find a quiet niche. It seems that their first child was born less than one year after that Peking spring.

The Mao-Yang match, in the spirit of May Fourth, was born of free choice by the two parties, which had been rare in old China. The actual ceremony of marriage, a year or so later in Changsha, meant so little to them that no one recalled it. Even Mao, talking to Edgar Snow in 1936, could not put an accurate date on it.

Miss Zhao in Changsha had not lived to carry forward May Fourth values. Miss Yang opted for a struggle to express them in a political movement. The dead Miss Zhao had stirred Mao's pen; the living Miss Yang stirred his loins. Yang redeemed Zhao's suicide, joining flesh with spirit, helping Mao during the 1920s to match the pen with the gun.

MAO TURNS TO MARXISM

At his incense table in the lama temple Mao read the *Communist Manifesto* (in translation, as he had to read everything that mattered to him). This time the ideas of Marx and Engels hit home. It was partly that the *Manifesto*—the first part of it appeared in Chinese in November 1919—was the most compelling of the Marxian works so far in Chinese. It was partly that the Russian Revolution, as analyzed by Professor Li Dazhao and others, had put a new sheen on Marxism in the eyes of a Chinese.

Russia became a beacon for Mao, as France was for English radicals of the 1790s. The theories of Marx he grasped only gradually. But the Bolshevik success got to his gut. . . .

Marxism is never merely transmitted, like an instruction or a disease, from one historical situation to another. It is reborn in the new place. So in Mao's case. The mental seeds of his brand of Marxism existed as he became a pro-liberation child of *New Youth* magazine from 1916. Marxism as a live hope for revolution in China came as a vision from St. Petersburg. Assimilation of the doctrines of Marx and Engels and Lenin occurred only as a third stage.

"Three books especially deeply carved my mind," said Mao of his second winter in Peking, "and built up in me a faith in Marxism." As well as the *Manifesto* there was one of Kautsky's works and *History of Socialism*, by Kirkup. The second two did not give Mao a very pure dose of Marxism.

But Mao had the "faith." From the summer of 1920 he considered himself a Marxist and thereafter he never wavered from that self-identification. Anarchism, reformism, utopianism, were all squeezed out as frameworks for his political thought. . . .

Mao tried to enlist Chen Duxiu's help on Hunan issues, but the revolutionary professor had bigger matters on hand. Russian advisers had arrived in China, sent by the newly founded Communist International, to consult Li and Chen about concrete steps toward a Bolshevik organization in China.

Chen was that spring the greatest single Marxist influence Mao ever knew. "His own assertions of belief," Mao said later of this ex-Peking iconoclast, "deeply impressed me at what was probably a critical period in my life." No doubt the laundry added to Mao's Marxist education by helping him see what Marx meant by the term "proletariat.". . .

MAY FOURTH PROJECTS IN CHANGSHA

A virtual civil war had been going on in Hunan, but in the summer of 1920 it ended with the ouster of Zhang by the more progressive Tan Yankai. Mao went back to Changsha full of political plans to take advantage of a newly liberal mood.

The man Tan chose to take over the troubled First Teachers' Training School happened to be one of Mao's old teachers. This educator soon made Mao director of [First Teachers' Training School] FTTS's primary school, Xiu Ye, where he had taught a class while editing *Xiang River Review*. Moreover, now that Cai Hesen and other Hunan stars were busy in French factories, Mao was unchallenged leader of the New People's Study Society.

The pay was good at Xiu Ye and the directorship had prestige. Mao quickly showed that he did not value austerity for its own sake. He settled with Miss Yang into Clear Water Pond house, a quiet and elegant ex-landlord's residence set in a garden. The rent was twelve dollars a month, the same as his entire wage at the Shanghai laundry, 50 percent above his wage at the library of Peking University. In outward trappings Mao was part of the Changsha establishment.

The period 1920–21 was a time of aligning thought and action. It brought a new focus to his political life. It also brought pain to certain of his relationships.

He pushed ahead with May Fourth kinds of projects. He started a Young People's Library and (with others) put back together the United Students' Association of Hunan. Visiting Music Mountain for a few weeks, he brought the torch of New Culture to his home county by establishing an Education Promotion Society. He wrote and edited at *Popular Daily*, a semiofficial educational organ, after a friend of his, He Shuheng, gained control of it and pulled it to the left.

Helped by a young woman he liked—another of Professor Yang's best students—Mao set up a Cultural Bookstore to seed Hunan with left-wing literature. "The people of Hunan are more starved in the mind than in the stomach," ran Mao's announcement about the shop.

Mao wangled three rooms at low rent for the Cultural Bookstore from Yale-in-China. He received financial support from Kaihui's mother. He even got warlord Tan to write the signboard for the shop in his fine brush strokes, and to preside over the opening ceremony. Subversion and the status quo rubbed shoulders for an afternoon.

The bookstore did well and grew seven branches in other towns. In its early days the best-selling items (all in Chinese) included Kirkup's *History of Socialism,* a pamphlet that introduced Marx's *Capital, A Study of the New Russia,* and the magazines *New Youth, New Life, New Education,* and *Labor Circles.*

Mao added pro-Russia spice to May Fourth themes. With He Shuheng of *Popular Daily* he started a Russian Affairs Study Group and a scheme for work-study in Russia. Under the influence of his Marxist faith, he tried to get a handle on labor union organizing. Prompted by Comintern advice, which reached him by letter from Shanghai and Peking, he began a Communist cell. Also a branch of the Socialist Youth Corps, an anteroom for looking over potential Communists.

When He Shuheng was fired from the Education Bureau in May 1921, and the radicals at *Popular Daily* were booted out with him. Mao appointed many of them as teachers in his own primary school. If there was a strike, students made up its core. Schoolteachers were the red thread holding together the broadening flaps of Mao's Marxist tent.

FTTS itself was crucial to the network. Mao recruited new followers by the month from its classrooms, relied on its salaries for the bread and butter of several co-leaders, used the fine facilities of its Alumni Association for meetings, raised gifts of ten dollars a head there for his Cultural Bookstore, and had young people going in and out of its library as if it were a bus station. FTTS was like an extended family for Mao the budding Communist.

Mao Turns to Communism

Alain Bouc

French scholar and journalist Alain Bouc takes up
Mao's story after his sojourn in Beijing. It was in
Beijing that Mao was first introduced to Marxism
and Communism. In this selection from his book on
Mao's political philosophy, Bouc describes the evolution of Mao's thinking, and his initiation into political writing and organizing.

Mao worked briefly with the Guomindang (Kuomintang) Nationalist Party before retreating to Hunan
where he studied the condition of Chinese peasants.
His understanding of the rural peasant would become the basis of his politic thought and future strategy. In 1927, Mao retreated to a rural mountainous
region in southeastern China where he implemented
many of his ideas in the Communist-controlled
Jiangxi Soviet. By then Mao had become completely
committed to communism as the solution to China's
problems.

In the autumn of 1918 Mao Tse-tung received his degree and
left for Peking. For several months he had a small job in the
university library. There he met the most prominent intellectuals of the extreme Left of the time, including his superior Li Ta-chao [Li Dazhao], the head librarian and a translator of Marxist works into Chinese. Little by little Mao gave
up his anarchist tendencies in favor of Marxism. In this
same year, at the age of twenty-five, he fell in love with the
charming Yang K'ai-hui, the daughter of one of his former
professors in Changsha. He married her three years later.

Mao returned to his province in 1919 and threw himself
more directly into politics by publishing the *Hsiang [Xiang]
River Review*. This journal appeared in July and was banned

Alain Bouc, *Mao Tse-Tung: A Guide to His Thought*, translated by Paul Auster and Ly-
dia Davis. New York: St. Martin's Press, 1977. Copyright © 1977 by Alain Bouc. Reproduced by permission of the publisher.

one month later by the governor of Hunan. In three of the four issues that appeared, Mao Tse-tung expressed his beliefs of the moment—the ideas of a lively young man who retained several general themes from Marxism and combined them with his own reflections. His first important article was "The Great Union of the Popular Masses.". . .

During the period immediately after World War I, Chinese youth were looking beyond China to foreign countries. They studied the Bolshevik revolution; they rebelled against the dealing at Versailles and the gifts offered to Japan by the West. In the large "May 4th Movement" of 1919, workers joined the angry students in demanding respect for territorial sovereignty and for the dignity of China. The towns were seething with excitement. At the end of the year Mao Tse-tung organized a student strike at Changsha directed against the governor of Hunan. Mao had to leave the province immediately and went to Peking and Shanghai. Previously he had declared himself an idealist, but as he later confided to [journalist] Edgar Snow, by 1920 he had become "in theory and to some extent in action, a Marxist."

In the autumn, having returned to Changsha, he established a Communist cell and a branch of the Youth League. He had just discovered the *Communist Manifesto* and Kautsky's *Class Struggle*. Now the principal of an elementary school, he expanded his political activities, started a bookstore, and became involved in the workers' movement of Hunan.

FOUNDING THE CHINESE COMMUNIST PARTY

In July 1921 Mao's ardent radicalism qualified him to be included in the founding of the Chinese Communist Party (CCP), which met for five days in a small school for girls in a district of Shanghai. He took control of the Party organization of Hunan, whose influence extended as far as the large coal mines of Anyuan in the neighboring province of Kiangsi. At that time the Communists in the region numbered only in the dozens, and Mao devoted much of his time to union-organizing activities. In September 1922 the miners of Anyuan, organized by Mao Tse-tung, Liu Shao-ch'i [Liu Shaoqi]—future Chief of State—and Li Li-san—future leader of the "hard" line [and labor organizer]—achieved very successful results with a strike which has remained famous. During the Cultural Revolution it was said that Mao and Liu had opposing ideas about union organization. Certain anti-Communist historians give all the credit for organizing that early strike to Li Li-san [later, CCP Secretary]. The matter is not clear. But several facts are beyond dispute: (1) Mao Tse-tung and his brother Mao Tse-min participated actively in the movement; (2) Mao Tse-tung had been in contact with the miners as early as autumn of the previous year; (3) the September 1922 strike involved 17,000 workers, including the railwaymen of the P'inghsiang line; and (4) the miners of Anyuan later formed the nucleus of the 2nd Regiment of the First Army based in the mountain range known as the Chingkongshan (1928).

MAO IN THE GUOMINDANG

Mao Tse-tung entered the central committee of the Party at the time of the Third Congress (June 1923). He was given organizational duties. In order to carry them out he went to Shanghai and established himself there. That same year the Communists came to an agreement with Sun Yat-sen's Kuomintang [quomindang] about conditions for cooperation. They agreed to dual-party membership, and Mao Tse-tung began his career in the Kuomintang.

The Communists' objective was clear: an alliance with a large progressive party against the feudal forces would assure them a national dimension and allow them to consolidate their position in the country while awaiting the moment—which would come much later, once feudalism had been done away with—for criticizing the bourgeois positions of the Kuomintang and fighting to seize power themselves. This is the classic "united front" policy. So there is nothing dishonorable about Mao Tse-tung's short but brilliant career in the Kuomintang, and the apparently obligatory silence on this subject in the People's Republic is surprising.

In January 1924 Mao Tse-tung became an alternate member of the Central Executive Committee of the Kuomintang. He was a member of the Shanghai Bureau of the Kuomintang and in February became chief of its organization bureau in that city. As far as he was concerned, this meant the Communists had control of one of the key political posts in the nation. But many radicals within the Chinese Communist Party criticized this policy of cooperation with the Kuomintang. Perhaps that explains why Mao left this post in 1924. In November 1926, however, Mao Tse-tung rose in the hierarchy again: he became the *de facto* head of the Kuomintang's propaganda department.

COMMUNISTS IN RURAL AREAS

Meanwhile he and other Communists had turned their attention to developing ties with the rural areas. The Chinese Communist Party had "infiltrated" the Peasant Movement Training Institute in Canton, which was under *de jure* Kuomintang control. In a report made to the 2nd Congress of the Kuomintang in 1926 Mao Tse-tung insisted on the need to intensify work in the rural areas. The following month he joined the Committee for the Peasant Movement, most of whose members were Communist who hoped to impose their politics on the whole of the Nationalist organization. In May, he became the secretary of a committee by the same name formed within the Communist Party in Shanghai.

But the hopes which the Communists had placed in the Kuomintang soon evaporated. The two organizations fought for control of the United Front. Sun Yat-sen's successor, Chiang Kai-shek, whom the Communists were supporting in his struggle for national unity, tried to get rid of them. In March 1926 he imprisoned the Communist instructors at the Whampoa Military Academy, one of whom was Chou En-lai. In May, he forbade members of the Chinese Communist Party to occupy management positions in the commissions of the Kuomintang's Central Committee. Mao Tse-tung left the department of propaganda but kept his post at the Canton Peasant Institute. The Party was divided: the radicals wanted to break away, while the "right," including Ch'en Tu-hsiu [Chen Duxiu], gave in. Later, Mao Tse-tung would say that the 1927 massacres had opened his eyes to the nature of the Kuomintang, which might imply that in 1926 he still cherished some illusions about it. . . .

At the end of 1926, full of uncertainty, Mao Tse-tung decided on a brilliant move. He returned to Hunan for more than a month, in order to study five districts and his native town of Shaoshan. He brought back a document that aroused worldwide interest, the "Report on an Investigation of the Peasant Movement in Hunan," one of the most brilliant articles he had ever written and one in which his whole personality was already asserting itself.

The March 1927 report is one of the great documents of the socialist movement. For the first time, the peasants acquired the dignity of revolutionaries—on an equal standing, or almost so, with the urban proletariat. They were the principal strength of the revolution. Moscow published the document. Bukharin praised it in front of the Soviet Party's Central Committee when it met in May. Around the same time the Soviet Union printed several of P'eng P'ai's [Peng Pai, Communist organizer in Southern China] equally "heretical" reports. But the majority of the Chinese Communist Party was not in the least prepared to follow the movement, nor, of course, was the Kuomintang, whose rural support lay among the conservatives. In April, Chiang Kai-shek massacred the Shanghai Communists: the break had come, belated and bloody.

MAO IN JIANGXI

Mao Tse-tung quarreled with his party. He left the Fifth Congress, in May 1927, discouraged at having his ideas about the peasant movement rejected. He was not reelected to the Politburo. The Leftist faction of the Kuomintang had dropped out of the Chinese Communist Party, which went underground and began to organize a series of revolts. Shortly after the Nanchang insurrection, a plan for revolt by units of the Nationalist army, which occurred in early August and marked the birth of the Red Army, the Chinese Communist Party changed leadership and Mao Tse-tung once again became a member of the Politburo. After the failure of the so-called "Autumn Harvest Uprising in Hunan," (September 1927) he led what remained of his troops— about one thousand men—up into the Chingkang Mountains. The saga of the underground began. It was to continue until the taking of power.

The Party was in upheaval. Mao was accused of Leftist adventurism. He was condemned by the Party in Hunan as well as by the Politburo and the International. Nevertheless, other troops made their way to the mountains of Kiangsi [Jiangxi], notably those of Chu Tehand [Zhe De, military leader] P'eng Teh-huai [Peng Dehuai, military leader]. In June 1928 the wind changed direction: few thousand ill-equipped soldiers won their first victory. Mao Tse-tung, in charge of the political leadership of the troops, stressed the importance of ideology. He and Chu Teh defined the principles of people's war ("Why Is It That Red Political Power Exists in China?" etc.). A series of defeats while carrying out the orders of the Politburo to attack towns induced them to break with the "putschist" line once and for all. The base of

Communist power in 1931 lay far from the towns. The Red Army drove back the troops of the Kuomintang, which tried three times to wipe it out. In 1931 the first All-China Soviet Congress proclaimed the establishment of the Chinese Soviet Republic, and Mao Tse-tung was elected Chairman. He became "Chairman Mao."

Most of the leaders of the Chinese Communist Party joined this little Republic, but not without challenging the authority of its head. At that time even Chou En-lai often sided with the group of students who had returned from Moscow, and for a time he replaced Mao in the army's political commissariat. For several years Mao Tse-tung did not write—or at least did not publish—anything of primary importance. In some sense he was pushed to the side. This was undoubtedly the darkest period of his career, even though he was still officially Chairman of the Republic.

CHAPTER 2

A LEADER EMERGES

The Jiangxi Soviet

J.A.G. Roberts

After 1927, Chinese Communists were under assault. The Nationalist (Guomindang) government led by Chiang Kai-shek was determined to eliminate them from the political scene. Mao and other Communists fled to the mountains of southeastern China and set up the Jiangxi Soviet, a region governed according to Communist principles. These principles, reviewed here by British scholar J.A.G. Roberts, included land reform and social reform, especially concerning the position of women in Chinese society. Another key principle was the formation and development of a disciplined Red Army. Eventually Chiang attacked the Jiangxi Soviet in a series of military "encirclements." The Communists were forced to flee in what came to be known as the Long March. J.A.G. Roberts is the author of several books on Chinese history and is Principal Lecturer at the University of Huddersfield.

After the failure of the Autumn Harvest uprising [rebellion ordered by Comintern, international Communists, and led by Mao] Mao Zedong had retreated to the mountain range on the borders of Hunan and Jiangxi known as the Jinggangshan, where he joined up with two bandit chiefs. In April 1928 Zhu De brought in the survivors from the attack on Nanchang. Later Peng Dehuai, a future minister of defence, arrived with a group from Hunan. These forces, the nucleus of the Red Army, were soon called into action to repel Guomindang attacks. Before the end of the year Mao had concluded that the Jinggangshan area was too small and too rugged to be a suitable base area, and in January 1929 he moved east to Ruijin in southern Jiangxi.

The Ruijin area became the most important of several Communist rural bases. For Mao Zedong, possession of a

J.A.G. Roberts, *A Concise History of China.* Cambridge, MA: Harvard University Press, 1999. Copyright © 1999 by J.A.G. Roberts. All rights reserved. Reproduced by permission.

rural base was an essential part of his revolutionary strategy. He likened a base to a person's buttocks—without buttocks one would be unable to sit down and regain one's strength. At the Ruijin base he began to put into practice three key policies, the first of which was to make the Red Army a disciplined and politicized force. Already at Jinggangshan Mao had enunciated the basic principles of guerrilla warfare: 'The enemy advances, we retreat; The enemy camps, we harass; The enemy tires, we attack; The enemy retreats, we pursue', and had required every soldier to know the Three Rules: to obey orders, to take nothing from the peasants, and to pool all captured goods. However, it was evident from remarks made by Mao at the Gutian conference held in December 1929 that many Red Army soldiers still lacked discipline and did not understand the aims of the revolution or the role that the army was expected to play. In future, political officers were appointed to help the army mobilize the masses and set up new regimes. At least one in three soldiers had to be a Party member. The army was intended to be democratic, the soldiers wore no badges of rank, all received the same way and all shared in the discussion of any proposed action.

The second policy concerned revolutionary land reform, that is the confiscation of land from landlords and its redistribution to poor peasants. This policy had only been adopted by the Chinese Communist Party (CCP) at its Fifth Congress in April 1927, on the eve of its split with the Guomindang, and there was no agreed line on whether land should also be confiscated from rich peasants, that is peasants who owned more land than they could farm with their own labour. At the Ruijin base Mao Zedong introduced a moderate policy which allowed rich peasants to retain their land. Villages were encouraged to form revolutionary committees, which first classified the inhabitants of the village as landlord, rich peasant, middle peasant and poor peasant and then applied the agreed redistribution of land.

The third policy concerned social reform and in particular the position of women in Chinese society. At the time of the May Fourth Movement Mao Zedong had criticized arranged marriages and during his investigation of the peasant movement in Human he had written approvingly of the formation of women's associations which challenged the authority of husbands. In 1930 he carried out a study of Xunwu in south-east Jiangxi to provide himself with recent and detailed information on a rural community. Among the matters he studied was the effect of permitting freedom of marriage and divorce. In his report he argued that male peasants opposed the emancipation of women only because they were uncertain of the outcome of land reform.

LAND REFORM

Mao's position in the Jiangxi soviet was unchallenged until 1931, when members of the Central Committee abandoned their undercover existence in Shanghai and moved to Ruijin. Later that year the Chinese Soviet Republic was established at Ruijin, with Mao Zedong its first president, although his authority and policies were now being challenged by the Twenty-eight Bolsheviks [Chinese Communists trained in Moscow]. The Soviet Republic immediately passed a radical land law which provided for the confiscation not only of landlords' land but also the land of rich peasants. It also approved a marriage law which defined marriage as 'a free institution between a man and a woman'. Both men and women could apply for a divorce and divorced women were given some economic protection. There immediately followed a spale of divorce petitions.

The survival of the rural soviets was threatened by developments from both within and without. In December 1930 the Nationalist Army made its first determined attack on the Communist bases in southern Jiangxi, but was forced to withdraw. The attack coincided with the Futian Incident, which involved the alleged infiltration of the Jiangxi action committee by the pro-Guomindang Anti-Bolshevist League. There followed a mutiny in a Red Army until and a purge by Mao Zedong of his suspected opponents. In July 1931 Jiang Jieshi [Chiang Kai-shek] took personal command of the Nationalist forces investing the Communist bases, which now numbered 300,000 men, and he was making good progress when the campaign was called off because of the Japanese occupation of Manchuria. This respite, and a Comintern declaration that the world depression would lead to a world revolutionary upsurge, encouraged the Twenty-eight Bolsheviks to denounce Mao Zedong's tactics of mobile guerrilla warfare as over-cautious. Mao lost his place on the Party's Military Council and the strategy promoted by Zhou Enlai of positional warfare and capturing cities was adopted.

In the Jiangxi central base the CCP had begun to apply its revolutionary land policy. Many landlords were dispossessed and others were killed, but it soon became apparent that some landlords and rich peasants were concealing the extent of their land-holdings. In June 1933 a Land Investigation movement was launched, originally with Mao Zedong's support, to identify cases of evasion. Later Zhang Wentian, one of the Twenty-eight Bolsheviks, took charge and the investigation became increasingly oppressive. In November 1933 the Guomindang Nineteenth Route Army, stationed in Fujian province, mutinied in protest against Jiang Jieshi's failure to oppose Japanese encroachment on China. Whereas Zhou Enlai was in favour of assisting the rebels, Mao Zedong counselled caution. While the Communist leadership was arguing, Jiang Jieshi stepped in and crushed the mutiny and a great opportunity for the Communists was lost.

NATIONALISTS ATTACK JIANGXI COMMUNISTS

In October 1933 Jiang Jieshi commenced his fifth encirclement campaign. This comprised both a major military offensive and a comprehensive political campaign. The Nationalist Army, which now numbered over 750,000 men in the field, was supported by German advisers and equipped with heavy guns and aeroplanes. To counter the Communist tactic of mobile warfare it had ringed the Jiangxi central base with 15,000 blockhouses. On the political front the Guomindang attempted to match CCP propaganda by requiring the officers in its armies to wear the same uniform and eat the the same food as their men. The population of the areas around the Communist bases was required to support a blockade of all essential supplies. It was at Nanchang in 1934, while he was planning the fifth extermination campaign, that Jiang Jieshi launched the New Life Movement [reformist ideology based on traditional Confucian values], which was in part a response to the threat of Communism.

THE LONG MARCH

The CCP's decision to abandon the Jiangxi base and set out on the Long March was probably taken in May 1934, although the departure was delayed until October. The main reason for going was the deteriorating military situation, although it has been suggested that the over-zealous application of the Land Investigation movement had lost the Party much popular support. Approximately 86,000 people set out from the Jiangxi base while some 20,000 sick and injured and a force of 30,000 soldiers remained behind. After breaking through the Guomindang blockade with surprising ease, the Red Army marched due west and crossed into Hunan and then Guangxi. The first major engagement was the crossing of the Xiang river north-east of Guilin, where the Red Army lost about half its strength. In January 1935 the Communists captured Zunyi in northern Guizhou and there an important conference took place. The main issue was the military failure which had resulted in the abandonment of the Jiangxi base. The policies pursued by the Politburo and by the military leadership, which included Otto Braun, the Comintern military adviser, were criticized and by implication those advocated by Mao Zedong were endorsed. Although Mao did not become Party leader at this point, his rise to power had begun.

The marchers left Zunyi with the intention of joining up with Zhang Guotao's Fourth Front Army, which had moved from its original base in Anhui to Sichuan. Various final destinations were under discussion, with Mao Zedong proposing moving north to oppose the Japanese. First the upper waters of the Yangzi river had to be traversed, which meant marching far to the west to shake off the Nationalists, and finally crossing the Jinsha or Golden Sands river. The marchers then turned north, through areas inhabited by sometimes hostile minority groups. Then came the most celebrated incident of the march, the crossing of the Dadu river by the Luding Bridge, an ancient chain suspension bridge guarded by a Guomindang machine-gun post. The next obstacle was the Great Snowy Mountain, where hundreds of men died from exposure. In June the two main branches of the Red Army met at Mao'ergai in north Sichuan. On the surface the reunion between Mao Zedong and Zhang Guotao was cordial, but past differences and political rivalries soon appeared and whereas Zhang Guotao chose to move west to Xizang, Mao Zedong continued northwards through Gansu, where he encountered one final physical challenge, the vast swamp of the Great Grasslands.

In October 1935 Mao Zedong and the First Front March reached the north Shaanxi rural base. The Long March had extended over 5000 miles and less than 20,000 of those who had set out arrived at its final destination. Many years later Mao Zedong was to speak sadly of the thousands who died, and the obligation felt by the survivors that their sacrifice should not have been in vain. As a result of the march the main theatre of Communist operations was transferred from the south to the north.

The Long March

Dick Wilson

Guomindang leader Chiang Kai-shek's military campaigns against the Jiangxi Soviet forced the Communists to flee for their lives. In 1934, they left their mountain stronghold and began an arduous retreat that would become legendary in Chinese history. The retreat, known as the Long March, took the Communists from southeastern China along a wandering route that would end six thousand miles and a year later in Yanan, in the north of China.

The suffering endured by the Communists was tremendous and those who survived the Long March were forever admired. Of the one hundred thousand that began the journey, only about five thousand survived to arrive in Yanan. Along the way, Mao Zedong emerged as the clear leader of the demoralized Communist movement. His personal charisma and vision, as well as his willingness to suffer with them, provided the Communists with the leadership they needed. In this selection from his biography of Mao, Dick Wilson describes the Long March and the emergence of a leader. Wilson is a journalist, scholar, and lecturer at the University of London. He is the author of numerous books and articles on China.

'Mao and about twenty others', his orderly recalled, 'left Yutu by the north gate, and then turned to the left towards the river which was all yellow, roaring and foaming, as though calling on the armies to advance. Soon the sun set and gusts of bitter wind chilled us. The Chairman wore a grey cloth uniform and an eight-cornered military cap, with no overcoat. He walked with enormous strides along the riverbanks.' It was five o'clock on an October [1934] evening and the 6000-mile epic which came to be known as the Long March had begun.

Dick Wilson, *Mao: The People's Emperor.* London: Hutchinson & Company, 1979. Copyright © 1979 by Dick Wilson. All rights reserved. Reproduced by permission.

But most of the time Mao, described as 'thin and emaciated' after his fever, 'had to ride because he was sick,' his orderly explained. The horse was still Mao's favourite dun-coloured steed which had been captured six years before. In addition to Chen, the orderly, Mao's party included his second wife, Ho Tzu-chen [He Zizhen (1909–1984)], in spite of her being several months pregnant; the male nurse, Chung Fu-chang, who had been assigned to Mao during his malaria; and a secretary, Huang Yu-fang.

But his two children by Ho Tzu-chen were too young to go and had to be left with peasant families in Kiangsi [Jiangxi]. They were never heard of again, though Mao had the army search the area when it came back fifteen years later. His youngest brother Tse-tan was also left behind in the rearguard with his new wife (Ho Tzu-chen's sister). They were never to be seen alive by Mao again, but the middle brother Tse-min came on the Long March as treasurer in charge of the base area government's money, bullion and machinery.

The Long March was, Mao later declared, 'our worst period . . ., blocked in front and pursued from behind.' He compared the loss of the Kiangsi base with the failure of the 1905 revolution in Russia. On another occasion he asserted that the Long March had been 'entirely unnecessary', since, better generalship could have defeated the fifth encirclement [attacks by Nationalists led by Chieng Kai-Shek].

RED ARMY GOALS

The Red Armies did not really know where they were heading. When Mao was asked later about their goals when the March began, he replied: 'If you mean, did we have any exact plans, the answer is that we had none. We intended to break out of the encirclement and join up with the other base areas. Beyond that, there was only a very deliberate desire to put ourselves in a position where we could fight the Japanese.'

It had not been at all certain that Mao would go on the Long March. If his malaria had not cleared up he might well have been left behind in the rearguard along with other sick leaders like Chu Chiu-pai (and, like them, captured by the Kuomintang). Even given his recovery, the feeling against him and his faction was running so strong within the leadership group that it is by no means impossible that they might have decided to dump him in Kiangsi. . . .

The first improvement in Mao's fortunes came after the

Red Army had broken out of the Kuomintang encirclement, at the cost of almost half its numbers, only to find its path to the nearest Communist base area, that of Ho Lung [Red Army general] 250 miles to the north, blocked by Chiang Kai-shek. Mao came forward with a plan to give up the attempt to join Ho Lung and to wheel instead toward Kwei-chow, where the enemy was weak. By following a long arc through Kweichow and over the Yangtze River, the Red Army would have a chance of reaching the Szechuan base of Chang Kuo-tao [Zhang guotao], Mao's old—and future—rival, without meeting Kuomintang forces. Mao's idea was accepted at a time when the military commanders were becoming doubtful about the generalship of [Otto] von Braun [Comintern military adviser] and Chou En-lai [Zhou Enlai, later Chinese premier].

The Red Army halted at Liping during the difficult crossing of Kweichow province, defended by troops of the Kwei-chow warlords, and a Politburo conference was held where the disagreements about military leadership came out into the open: Mao regained a *de facto* seat on the Central Committee. It was decided to continue to Tsunyi. During this stage of the Long March, Mao's wife, Ho Tzu-chen, was wounded in an attack by low-flying bombers. It was said that twenty pieces of shrapnel lodged in her body, and yet she lived on to give birth to another baby and complete the March. . . .

At Tsunyi, temporarily secure from attack, they were able to spend twelve days resting, recruiting new soldiers and arguing about their disagreements. An enlarged meeting of the Politburo was convened, in which the regular members were supplemented by a number of senior Central Committee members and by generals or political commissars. . . .

MAO TAKES TOP POST

Mao now became a member of the Politburo Standing Committee, since it had been the Party's habit for some years, in view of the importance of the armed struggle, to give the Chairman of the Revolutionary Military Council a seat on the Politburo Standing Committee. After his two years of demotion from the higher councils of the Party, this secured for Mao a position in the inner core of the Party leadership which he never again relinquished, and from which he was able to drive his way to the top ten years later. He was now indisputably one of the top five or six men in the Party. . . .

The talking over, Mao now concentrated on the military challenge ahead, relying heavily on Chou [Zhou Enlai] for organizational support and Liu Po-cheng for military planning. His forces had fallen to only 30,000 when they took Tsunyi, but 20,000 new soldiers were recruited in the city to bring the Red Army up to about 50,000. The problem was how to cross the heavily defended Yangtze [Chang Jiang] River to Chiang Kuo-tao's base in northern Szechuan. The first attempt took five weeks, but was unsuccessful, and Mao's men found themselves in Tsunyi again at the end of February. . . .

But then Mao heard on the Red Army's primitive radio that Chang Kuo-tao had been obliged, under enemy pressure, to abandon his Szechuan base and head west to a point where he could no longer help Mao's campaign to cross the Yangtze. In March Mao began a series of complex manoeuvres to get across on his own. He sent men to cross the Chihshui River for the third time, in order to mislead the Kuomintang into moving its forces to that stretch of the Yangtze's northern bank. But the Communists quickly turned about, recrossed the Chihshui and made a forced march south towards Kweiyang, capital of Kweichow province. It was concerning these back-tracking operations that recriminations surfaced forty years later about the alleged unwillingness of Generals Lin Piao and Peng Teh-huai to follow Mao's orders.

CROSSING RIVERS AND MOUNTAINS

By an intricate series of feints, forced marches and ruses, the Red Army eventually crossed the River Yangtze at Chiaochia, where the river is locally called the Chinsha River—River of Golden Sand—with fierce currents and treacherous navigation. The Communists succeeded in capturing half a dozen boats from the other side and were then able to ferry themselves across in small lots over nine successive days and nights. . . .

The crossing of the River of Golden Sand was owed to a combination of daring and good luck. But it is also likely that the local warlord was far from being a whole-hearted supporter of the Kuomintang, since he eventually rebelled against Chiang and was given honoured positions under the People's Republic after 1949: this was one of the provinces which the Kuomintang's forces could not enter under its complex political arrangements with various regional warlords.

Mao now came to a part of China totally unfamiliar to most Chinese. 'When we came to the south and crossed the Yangtze', he recollected afterwards, 'we ran into snakes, mosquitoes, scorching weather and a shortage of food.' . . .

The next hazard was to cross the Tatu River, a mountain torrent which provided the most difficult obstacle in the whole of the Long March. The Red Army attempted to cross it at Anshunchang, where the Taiping rebels of the nineteenth century had been defeated and where many heroes of *Romance of The Three Kingdoms* had fallen in battle.

By an incredible chance the enemy commander was on the south bank to feast with his wife's relatives, thinking that the Communists would take many more days to cover the ground from their previous known position. A Red detachment was able to capture him and his boat, and then cross and secure the other boats. The Red Army then began to cross, using the three ferry boats day and night for three days. But the onset of the spring waters (it was late May) made it increasingly difficult, taking more and more time on each crossing, and meanwhile Chiang's bombers were harassing them and enemy forces were racing in from at least two directions. They decided to march to the Luting bridge, further north, which would be their last chance to cross over into north China. In those despairing days Mao even discussed with von Braun the possibility of crossing Sikang and Chinghai to join with the Russians in Sinkiang: the German dissuaded him.

CAPTURE OF LUTING BRIDGE

The capture of the Luting bridge was another feat of heroism. This was a string of thirteen iron chains, across nine of which there were normally planks for walking—the other four protecting the crosser at the sides. When the Communists arrived, the enemy had cleared away more than half of the planks, assuming that no one would be so foolhardy as to try to cross on the chains alone. . . .

So Mao's soldiers did what was not expected of them. They crossed the chains dangling hand over hand, and although the men in front were inevitably shot, to fall into the wild torrent below, enough of them reached the north bridgehead to take it. By then the enemy had set fire to the planks left on their side, but even so the Communists were not stopped. Meanwhile, from behind, the Red Army engineers were laying tree trunks on the chains from the southern side as a new floor.

Mao watched the crossing with his heart in his mouth. One stick of dynamite at the moorings would have ended his career and his movement.

'After crossing the Tatu River,' Mao later recollected, 'where should we go? We racked our brains to make a decision.' In fact there was little choice: they had to continue northwards, skirting the edge of civilized China to reach the Shensi Red base. But the physical obstacles were formidable. The first of these was the Great Snow Mountain.

On the way they were suddenly dive-bombed by three enemy planes while crossing an open valley. The bodyguard standing next to Mao was hit, and lay silently, clutching his abdomen, while Mao bent over him.

'You'll be all right, comrade Hu Chang-pao,' Mao said, 'just keep quiet, and we'll carry you to Shuitseti, where we can get a doctor who will see to you.'

But the man's head fell over and his eyes closed. Mao slid out his arm from under him, where he had been cradling his head, and stood up. He laid a quilt over the body, and then they buried it. Mao had been inches from death.

The Red Army had to climb 16,000 feet in order to cross the Great Snow Mountain, and many of the men came to grief. Mao himself succumbed to malaria again and had to be carried on a stretcher for part of the way. . . .

MAO MEETS A RIVAL

Mao had his confrontation, in the unlikely foothills of Tibet, with his rival Chang Kuo-tao, leader of another Communist base area and Mao's equal in Party service, and the commanders of the Fourth Front Army. They had retreated to the western regions two years earlier. The reunion took place on 20 July in the village of Lianghokou, in the pouring rain.

That night General Chu Teh walked back with Chang to his quarters, and talked with him until dawn, explaining that the Tsunyi decisions had been taken at a time of pressing difficulty when Mao had offered an initiative at a moment of crisis and was elected to assume responsibility in the Party to resolve the dispute within its leadership. Chu urged Chang to stick to the military agenda for the immediate future and not to bring up political questions.

But Chang could hardly fail to take heart from the compar-

THE LONG MARCH

ison between his army and Mao's. They may have been about equal in numbers, possibly as much as 45,000 each, but the Fourth, not having had to fight with Chiang Kai-shek's crack troops, and having had a good rest, was in far better shape, better fed, better clothed and better equipped. One of the Long Marchers commented of the Chang force: 'They acted like rich men meeting poor relatives.' After the feasting and public speeches, the leaders went into stormy private debate at a Politburo conference. Chang's idea of retreating further west towards Sinkiang, where Russian support would be available, was rejected. He made the mistake of defying both the Twenty-Eight Bolsheviks [Moscow-trained Chinese Communists] and the Maoists at the same time, as well as pressing his claims to be the Party's General Secretary.

Mao, knowing that Lin Piao and other generals were not fully satisfied with his own leadership, confessed afterwards that this confrontation with Chang Kuo-tao was 'the darkest moment of his life', when the break-up of the Party and even civil war amongst its leaders 'hung in the balance'. But a majority of his own First Army colleagues and the Politburo members who had been with him on the Long March from

Kiangsi accepted his own plan to continue moving north towards Mongolia.

The two armies now joined but divided again into two columns of mixed units, one under Mao and the other under Chang. . . .

The two columns moved off at the beginning of August by different routes towards the north, but were suddenly separated by a river which swelled up into a raging torrent and defied passage. Chang declared that the river could not be crossed and that his column must therefore return to Sikang; Generals Chu Teh and Liu Po-cheng, together with the only radio generator in the army, would have to go with him. Chu and Liu refused, upon which Chang took General Chu prisoner and ordered him to denounce Mao and cut off relations with him.

'You can no more cut me off from Mao', Chu is supposed to have replied, 'than you can cut a man in half.'

To this Chang said that if General Chu refused to obey him, he would be shot.

'That is within your power,' Chu replied, 'I cannot prevent you. I will not obey your orders!'

But Chang did not carry out his threat, perhaps because the troops loyal to Chu would have risen against his own army. Rather than see this dreadful spectacle of two Communist armies at each other's throats, General Chu reluctantly agreed to turn back with Chang.

Chang's story is that he radioed Mao's column ordering him to halt, but Mao took his column on rather than go back to consult or help his comrades. Kuomintang reinforcements then came in to prevent Chang from following along Mao's route, so he swung south. In the end he was to keep his men for a whole year in the south-west before rejoining Mao and the others in Shensi.

CROSSING THE GRASSLANDS

Mao's column now spent six days crossing the Grasslands of Chinghai [Qinghai]. This is a high plateau about 8000 feet above the sea where it rains for most of the year (especially in August) and the drainage is poor. It has therefore become a vast swamp stretching for hundreds of miles without trees or shrubs, birds or insects, without even stones.

'If we turn south,' Mao briefed his officers, 'it means running away, and the end of the revolution. We have no choice but to go forward. Our enemies have assumed that we will move into eastern Szechuan rather than attempt the Grasslands road into Shensi and Kansu. But the enemy does not understand us at all. We purposely choose the path which he least expects us to take.'

The Red Army had to acquire food before going into the Grasslands, and took considerable amounts of wheat, sheep, cattle and turnips (each one big enough to 'feed fifteen men', according to Mao) from the tribesmen of this area.

'This is our only foreign debt,' Mao said humorously after reaching the Shensi base, 'and some day we must repay the Mantzu and the Tibetans for the provisions we were obliged to take from them.'

Mao's orderly recalled of the swamp itself: 'The sodden earth squelched monotonously, *pu-chih, pu-chih*, as we laboured over it. A careless step could send you to a fearful death in its muddy depths, trap your feet in a morass. Once caught it was difficult to pull your legs out of the quagmire without the help of your comrades.'. . .

At the end of October 1935 Mao and his Long Marchers came at long last to the town of Wuchichen in the Shensi soviet area. They stayed for the first time in caves cut in the side of the hills, mostly dismayed to find that even among friends there was no rice, only golden millet. Mao's cook served a leg of mutton ungarnished because he knew no way of cooking millet. 'Learn to do it,' said Mao when he heard of this, 'it isn't difficult. We've got to learn new ways of living when we come to a new place, otherwise we'll starve to death.'

Mao quickly led a party through falling snowflakes to Hsiashihwan, the headquarters of this Red base area, to meet its leaders. . . .

Of the 100,000 who had left Kiangsi almost exactly a year before, only about 5000 survived the full journey and emerged in Shensi foot-sore, bedraggled, starved and exhausted. They had eaten tree-bark and drunk their own urine; they had fought the sun and the rocks and the snow. They had crossed the morass and survived. Now the ordeal was over.

Mao's military leadership was vindicated; it remained for him to assert his claim to the political leadership. His own immediate assessment came in a famous poem called, simply, *The Long March:*

The Red Army fears not the trials of the Long March,
Holding light ten thousand crags and torrents.
The Five Ridges wind like gentle ripples
And the majestic Wumeng roll by, globules of clay.
Warm the steep cliffs lapped by the waters of Golden Sand,
Cold the iron chains spanning the Tatu River.
Minshan's 300 miles of snow joyously crossed,
The three Armies march on, each face glowing.

The outside world was astonished, and the supporters of the Communists delighted at the survival of Mao's band to fight another day.

Mao at Yanan

John King Fairbank

By 1937, the suffering of the Long March was over and the Communists set up a new base in rural Shaanxi Province at Yanan under the leadership of Mao Zedong. Here Mao had time to develop his own political thought and to reinterpret Marxism to fit the Chinese context. The political philosophy that merged came to be known as Mao Zedong Thought, or Maoism in the West. Reform principles seen earlier at the Jiangxi soviet were repeated here: social reform, land reform, and emphasis on the peasantry as a base of his political power in a doctrine known as the "mass line."

At the same time, Mao's reformism also extended to controlling the thought and writings of Chinese Communist intellectuals. Mao was determined early to require intellectuals to adhere to his version of the Chinese Communist Party doctrine. Those intellectuals who did not adhere suffered. Harvard scholar John King Fairbank reviews Mao's time in Yanan in this selection. Fairbank is the author of many books and articles on Chinese history.

To control and direct the widespread organization of the Chinese Communist Party (CCP) movement over the broad stretches of North China required dedicated and disciplined party members, experienced cadres (activists) in the villages, an attempt at self-sufficiency in each base, and the use of radio telegraphy to transmit messages. The principle of centralized control over a decentralized situation was exhibited in the government organization. The Central Committee of the party had its departments at Yan'an [Yanan] dealing with military affairs, organization, united-front work, enemy-occupied areas, labor, women, and the like, a total of twelve categories. Meantime, the territorial organization was di-

John King Fairbank, *China: A New History.* Cambridge, MA: Belknap Press of Harvard University Press, 1992. Copyright © 1992 by the President and Fellows of Harvard College. All rights reserved. Reproduced by permission.

vided among half a dozen regional bureaus, such as North China, Northwest China, the Central Plain. Within these regional bureaus were staff sections corresponding to those under the Central Committee at Yan'an. The principle of "integration" (*yiyuanhua*) meant that all directives from the capital at Yan'an to the specialized staff sections of the regional bureaus must go through or at least be fully known to the branch bureau chief, as the local coordinator.

MAO'S GOALS AT YANAN

Yan'an in World War II became to a few foreign observers a never-never-land full of sunshine and bonhomie. The revolutionary enthusiasm was infectious, as Edgar Snow and other journalists reported to the world. The homespun democracy apparent among the CCP leaders was a startling contrast to Chongqing [nationalist headquarters]. American aid never really got to Yan'an, and the superficiality of contact allowed the cultivation of a mythology that captivated liberals abroad.

The secret of Mao's success at Yan'an was his flexibility at combining short-term and long-term goals. In the short term he espoused in 1940 the New Democracy as a united-front doctrine that would embrace all the Chinese people who would subscribe to CCP leadership. For the long term, he steadily developed the party organization, including its control over intellectuals. The Yan'an rectification movement of 1942–1944 (more fully described below) established the campaign style of mobilization, including individual isolation, terror, struggle, confession, humiliation, and subservience. Party members would come to know it well and, in time, so would the public. It was one of Mao's achievements, with roots both in Leninism—Stalinism and in Imperial Confucianism.

Meantime, the real sinews of power grew up in the CCP mobilization of the peasantry in North China. The Japanese were excellent targets to mobilize against. Invading China along the rail lines, they tried to seal off the areas in between, but their rail-line blockhouses could not control trade and contact across the lines. In general their invasion cultivated the ground for the CCP mobilization. Whether the CCP success in this situation was due to a simple nationalism or to CCP doctrine is essentially a nonquestion because the CCP already represented national communism, not the Comintern, while CCP doctrines grew out of practice in the villages and also enlisted intellectuals in a grand scheme of world salvation.

PRINCIPLES OF PARTY CONTROL

In the governments of the Border Region and Liberated Areas that the CCP developed in different parts of North China, the first principle was party control based on indoctrination of cadres and enforcement of discipline. The indoctrination had to combine Mao's long-term principles with his tactical flexibility, for the CCP-organized regimes operated at great distances from Yan'an and very much on their own except for unreliable radio communication.

The second principle was to find out what the peasants wanted and give it to them: first of all, local peace and order; second, an army of friendly troops who helped in peasant life, harvesting crops when necessary and fraternizing with the villagers; third, a recruitment of local activists who might very well be found at the upper level of the poor peasantry, people of ability who felt frustrated by circumstance; fourth, a program for economic betterment partly through improved crops but mainly through agricultural cooperation in the form of mutual aid, organized transport, and production of consumer goods in cooperatives.

As these efforts went forward, they became the basis for a third principle: class struggle. This had to be approached in a gingerly fashion because North China landlords were hardly more than rich peasants but might be able to field their own local forces drawn from secret societies and mercenaries. In the early years the Guomindang (GMD) also had its forces in parts of North China and so provided an alternative focus of allegiance. The CCP dealt with this by setting up the rather persuasive three thirds system: the Communists would control only one third of the small congresses that sanctioned local government, leaving the other two thirds to the GMD and independents. On this basis, of course, the CCP's superior discipline and dedication let them become leaders on their merits. As their good repute became justified in popular esteem, they could begin to prepare for land reform in addition to economic production programs.

LAND REFORM

Land reform could be pursued only after three ingredients were present: military control, economic improvement, and recruitment of village activists. In the process itself the trick was to mobilize opinion against landlord despots, such as they were, and—by denouncing or liquidating them—commit the villagers to a revolutionary course. All land-holdings were evaluated and redistributed on a more equal basis according to categories that gave each individual his status as a rich, middle, or poor peasant or landless laborer. If this redistribution could be made to stick, village activists could begin to be indoctrinated in the ethos of the party's leadership. The message was simply that the people could make a better future for themselves if they would organize their efforts in a new unity. The leadership of this new unity could be found in the CCP. While the individual could achieve nothing alone, he could contribute by sacrificing his individual interests to that of the common cause. The principle of democratic centralism was then extolled as a means whereby all could have their say and make their input, but once a party decision had been made, all would obey it. This would never have gone down in a New England town meeting, but in a North China village, where the alternative was government by landlords and officials from outside the region, it was properly persuasive.

In short, the idea of the "mass line" was here adumbrated: the party must go among the people to discover their grievances and needs, which could then be formulated by the party and explained to the masses as their own best interest. This from-the-masses to-the-masses concept was indeed a sort of democracy suited to Chinese tradition, where the upper-class official had governed best when he had the true interests of the local people at heart and so governed on their behalf.

In this way the war of resistance against Japan provided the sanction for a CCP mobilization of the Chinese masses in the countryside; and this, once achieved, gave a new power to the CCP based not on the cities but on the villages. CCP expansion and base-building across North China and even in the Yangzi region reached a new high point in 1940. . .

MAO'S ASCENDANCY IN THE PARTY

Meanwhile, the Communist expansion in the Yangzi region, particularly through the New Fourth Army [Communist rear guard left behind when the Red Army set off on the Long March], also aroused retaliation from Nationalist forces. Negotiations led to the withdrawal of most of the New Fourth

Army from south to north of the Yangzi, but in January 1941 the headquarters unit of several thousand CCP troops was ambushed by the Nationalists and practically destroyed in what was known as the "New Fourth Army incident." While neither party acknowledged the end of the united front, because it was advantageous to both of them in form, it nevertheless had become a fact.

These reverses left Yan'an facing a severe crisis. The GMD and Japanese blockades had cut off nearly all trade, inflation was rising rapidly, and the whole regime had to pull back to survive. While Yan'an had got along with very modest taxation of the peasant grain crop, by 1941 bad weather created shortages and the government began to demand some 10 percent of the grain produced. Confiscations from landlords had dried up. The only way out was to go for self-sufficiency, such as by local production of consumer goods like cotton cloth. Cultivated land and irrigation were greatly increased, the grain yield went up, and livestock were also increased. In short, the economic crisis was met by a great effort to raise production by all possible means.

Parallel with this economic recovery, the early 1940s at Yan'an saw Mao Zedong finally establish his ascendancy over the CCP. Mao's reading of Marxist works had not been extensive until he had some leisure time at Yan'an after 1936. Soon he was giving lectures on dialectical materialism and producing his essays "On Practice" and "On Contradiction." Because he had not yet eliminated the twenty-eight Bolsheviks, his lecturing was designed to show his capacity for intellectual leadership, even though the lectures were rather crude. Nevertheless, Mao showed his originality by his stress on contradictions, which was posited on the "unity of opposites," an idea with a long Chinese history behind it.

His philosophical aim at Yan'an was not merely to establish a nationalistic party concerned for the Chinese nation but also to adapt Marxism to Chinese uses. The political imperative was that the party had to achieve disciplined organization, marked by acceptance of the party line, so that party members could be counted on to operate at a distance in conformity with directives. The GMD had suffered from intense factionalism. The CCP at Yan'an as a smaller organization moved to eradicate it with some success.

Consensus among party activists depended on their being intellectually convinced of the wisdom of the CCP line. The line must invoke theoretical principles to sanction practical action. This was achieved by the gradual creation of the body of ideas popularly known in the West as Maoism but in Chinese more modestly called Mao Zedong Thought. It represented the sinification of Marxism—Leninism, the application of its universal principles to the specific conditions of China. How Mao built it up, piece by piece, is therefore an interesting question worth our pausing to examine.

MAO ZEDONG THOUGHT

Both Buddhism and Christianity when they came into China had faced a problem of terminology, how to pick Chinese characters that would express the new concepts but keep them distinct from old established Chinese concepts expressed in the same characters. Japanese socialists had pioneered in this effort. Long before Mao, the Chinese adaptation of Marxism had begun at the level of translation of key terms. Marx's "proletariat," the key actor in his cosmic drama, was certainly associated in Western thinking with urban life, specifically early nineteenth-century factory workers in the often unspeakable conditions of Western European industrialization. The translation into Chinese, however, produced the term *wuchan jieji,* meaning "propertyless class," in other words, the very poor who might be either in the city or the countryside, and of course in China were mainly in the countryside. In effect, the European "proletariat" were automatically to be found in China in the poor "peasantry" among the farmers and landless laborers. Granted that Marxist terminology was used by Chinese Marxists in terms consonant with those of Moscow Marxists, there was nevertheless a subtle difference when they spread their doctrine to the Chinese students and common people.

The Chinese term used for "feudal," *fengjian,* had referred in classic Chinese thinking to the fragmentation of sovereignty in the period of Warring States before the Qin unification in 221 BC. It meant simply decentralized administration, without reference to the land system or the status of the cultivators. However, if feudalism was to be identified in China with landowner exploitation, as Communists wished to do, then feudalism had gone on in China a couple of thousand years. Thus the periods that Marx defined for European history could not be easily applied to China. If all of Chinese history for 2,000 years after 221 BC had been "feudal," the term lost meaning or was humiliating. "Proletariat" and "feudal" were only two of the key terms of Marxism, and they obviously did not fit the Chinese scene without really being bent out of shape.

Quite aside from this terminological problem in sinification, the economic foundation of Chinese life, being mainly in the countryside, gave the Chinese revolution necessarily a rural character more pronounced than that in the Soviet Union. The peasantry had to be the chief revolutionists. The final factor making for sinification was the overriding sentiment of Chinese nationalism based on cultural and historical pride, which meant China could not be the tail of someone else's dog. In effect, the Chinese people could accept only a Chinese Marxism.

In time Chinese historical consciousness would undermine the verisimilitude of Marxism in China. But for Mao's purposes it could be asserted that the domination of the landlord class ("feudalism") was backed by the "imperialist" exploiters from abroad, while the rise of a Chinese merchant class centered in towns produced a capitalist "national bourgeoisie." Only its "comprador" wing sold out to the "imperialist" exploiters, and the situation might be cured by an establishment of central state authority to complete the tasks of the "bourgeois-democratic revolution." Later the revolution would reach the final stage of socialism. In other words, there was enough fit to enable Marxism to get on with the job of revolution by propagating its new world-historical belief system. . . .

THE RECTIFICATION CAMPAIGN OF 1942–1944

Now that he was in power, Mao pushed not only to consolidate his position but to unify the party and to ensure discipline. The rectification campaign of 1942–1944 was limited to party members, who had increased in number and lacked the cohesion of the Long March generation. The targets of the campaign were "subjectivism, sectarianism, and party formalism." "Subjectivism" targeted dogmatists who could not combine theory with practice. "Sectarianism" referred to the recent factionalism and the inevitable cleavages between soldiers and civilians, party and nonparty, old and new party members, and so on. "Party formalism" meant the use of jargon instead of practical problem-solving. Other evils were those of creeping bureaucratism and routinization of administration. These could be combatted partly by decentralization—transferring officials down to work in villages closer to practical problems. Also attacked was the individualism of the many intellectuals who had come to Yan'an from the coastal cities.

One principal factor made for friction in the CCP's relationship with intellectuals. Whereas scholars under the imperial order had been oriented toward public service, the writers of the twentieth-century revolution had focused on evils and misdemeanors of government because they had grown up as a class divorced from office-holding. The traditional literati, in short, had now been split into two groups, those in public service and those in public criticism. The modern intellectuals were in the tradition of remonstrance, pointing out the inadequacies of the authorities. Since that great critic of the GMD, Lu Xun, had died in 1936, his name could be safely invoked as that of a paragon.

In Yan'an in the early 1940s the control of literature by the new state authority of the CCP became a central issue. Sino-liberal patriots of all sorts had joined the revolution, and their commitment to attack the imperfections of the GMD naturally led them on to criticize the emerging imperfections of the CCP. Lu Xun's closest followers had continued under the CCP to voice their criticisms. When Mao Zedong gave his two lectures on literature and art at Yan'an early in 1942, he laid down the law that literature should serve the state, in this case the cause of CCP-led revolution. It should therefore be upbeat in the style of socialist realism from the Soviet Union and avoid the kind of revelation of evils and inadequacies that had been a Communist specialty in the GMD period.

THOUGHT REFORM

The methods whereby Mao's thought-reform movement was carried out at Yan'an in 1942–1944 would become very familiar in CCP history from then on. The individual whose thoughts were to be reformed was first investigated and persuaded to describe himself and his life experience to the point where the group could begin to criticize him. In study-group criticism the individual was at once isolated and subjected to the rebukes or admonishments of everyone else. This shook his self-confidence. As a next step, in public struggle meetings the individual was publicly accused and humiliated before a large and usually jeering audience representing the community. At this point another factor operated, namely, the dependence of the Chinese individual upon group esteem as well as the approval of authority.

As the pressure increased and the individual found no escape from the denigration of his old self, he was led into writing confessions to analyze his evil conduct and his desire to change. Pressure was increased if he was then isolated in jail—subjected to solitary confinement or placed in a cell with others and obliged to wear paper handcuffs, which he could not break without dire consequences. The consequent obliteration of his personality thus prepared him for the final stage of rebirth and reconciliation. When his confession was finally accepted and the party welcomed him back into the fold, he might experience a tremendous elation and willingness to accept the party's guidance. Whether this psychological experience did change personalities is less certain than the fact that it was a highly unpleasant experience to be avoided in the future. One way or the other, the result was conformity to the party line.

Lest we begin to believe in total power and total subjection, we must give due weight to the vigor of Chinese personalities. Those who stood forth as critics were frequently obdurate and essentially uncompromising individuals who felt duty-bound to stick to their principles and criticize evils. The widespread use of thought reform by the CCP thus should not necessarily be taken to mean that Chinese intellectuals were natural slaves. On the contrary, their independence of judgment was hard for the party to overcome. . . .

Mass-Line Doctrine

In 1943 Mao put forward his doctrine of the "mass line." Like many of Mao's intellectual formulations, this was double-ended and ambiguous so that it could be applied in either of two ways. While it asserted the need of consulting the masses and having a mass participation of some sort in the government, it also reaffirmed the necessity for central control and leadership. At any given time either one could be given the greater emphasis, just as *New Democracy* had provided a theoretical basis for joining with the GMD in a second united front or opposing the GMD as reactionary. Again, one's class status might be defined by reference to one's parents and economic livelihood or it could be defined by one's ideas and aspirations. Similarly, the people were enshrined as the final arbiters and beneficiaries of the revolution, but some persons could be labeled as enemies of the people. This could be done by administrative fiat from above.

It was typical of this line of development that Mao should define contradictions as being some of them antagonistic and some of them nonantagonistic, that is, arguable. Thus some contradictions made you an enemy of the people and some did not, depending on how you were perceived. All in all, it was a very flexible structure of ideas, as though Marx and Engels had been seduced by Yin and Yang. Once Mao had control over it, he was truly in a position of leadership. Unity resulted because those who held out against Mao were vilified, penalized, jailed, or even executed.

Civil War

Jerome Chen

Ridding China of Japanese invaders during World War II was the first priority of the Chinese Communists. When the war ended in 1945, the Communists and Nationalists turned on each other and began a fight to the death. The stakes were high because the victor would rule China. In this selection, British historian Jerome Chen, lecturer at the University of Leeds, recounts the events of China's civil war from 1946 to 1949.

The Nationalists led by Chiang Kai-shek, although far wealthier and better armed than the Communists, were plagued with corruption and inefficiency. The Chinese Communist Party led by Mao, continued to implement reform while developing a highly disciplined and well-regarded People's Liberation Army (PLA). When it had become apparent that the Communists had won the "war of liberation," Chiang and other Nationalists fled to Taiwan. On October 1, 1949, Mao Zedong announced the foundation of the People's Republic of China.

After the eight-year resistance against Japan, the people of China, heartily sick of war, were dragged into an internecine conflict for another four years. At the outset everyone counselled against it—[Soviet dictator Josef] Stalin wanted the Chinese Communist Party (CCP) to seek a *modus vivendi* [temporary arrangement] with Chiang [Kai-shek, Nationalist leader]; General George Marshall and the American military representatives argued that, in spite of its military preponderance, the KMT [guomindang (GMD) or Nationalist Party] could not destroy the communist movement by force and that the Chinese economy was unable to sustain another war and yet escape a total collapse; the United Kingdom Trade Mission of 1946–7 regarded peace as the first

Jerome Chen, *Mao and the Chinese Revolution*. London: Oxford University Press, 1965. Copyright © 1965 by Oxford University Press. All rights reserved. Reproduced by permission.

economic need of China. But Chiang believed that China, having an agrarian economy, did not have to fear an economic collapse in the foreseeable future and that the KMT could efface communism from the country by force. His Chief-of-Staff [Ho Yingchin] estimated that the KMT military strength was over eleven times as great as that of the CCP. Mao characterized this kind of assessment in these words:

> The enemy always underrates the energy of our army and overrates his own strength. . . .

But Chiang held fast to his belief until March 1948, for he, like the communists, regarded himself as a protagonist of a revolution whose triumph was pre-determined.

The foundations on which Chiang based his confidence were, perhaps, the numerical superiority of his troops, his own immense popularity as the man who led his country to victory, and the steadfastness of United States' friendship and aid. The U.S. aid was of particular importance; without it the KMT's fate was sealed and because of it Mao and the CCP felt a certain hostility towards America and attacked her in tones so acrimonious that they recoiled on their users. What the CCP accused the Americans of was what Chiang was hoping for—their direct involvement in the war, but the Americans themselves, apart from giving substantial assistance, refused actual participation. The defeat of Thomas E. Dewey in the 1948 [American] Presidential Election disappointed Chiang whose subsequent urgent appeal to President Truman for military aid and the appointment of American officers to command the KMT troops was coldly received. Even Madame Chiang's visit to the U.S. at the end of 1948, aiming at an alliance against the communists, resulted only in humiliation. . . .

MAO AS LEADER

In contrast to the intemperate but sartorially immaculate Chiang Kai-shek, whose actual leadership Mao openly doubted for the first time in September 1946, Mao Tse-tung remained informal in dress in spite of the personality cult that grew round him, but impressed his visitors as benign and calm. The brown tunic he wore at the press conference in Chungking on 29 August 1945 he was still wearing when [journalist] Robert Payne saw him in 1946 and when [author] Yüan Hsüeh-k'ai met him on the eve of his departure from Yenan in March 1947. Still free from mannerisms, he had changed some of his old habits, eating less pepper, smoking fewer cigarettes, and going to bed earlier at night, with the result that he put on some weight. His long, thick hair was still black, crowning his high and bronzed forehead. Before leaving Yenan on 18 March 1947, he still lived in the same cave-like dwelling where he had received [journalist] Gunther Stein and other visitors. The sofa with fiendish springs, the chair, and the rickety table were there, too. Prominent on the wall was a map bearing numerous pencil marks in blue and red.

His food remained frugal, consisting normally of potatoes, turnips, and cabbage, some meat, and millet or steamed wheat buns. But in the minds of his followers, a strong personality cult centering on this simple-living man had become deep-rooted . . . .

Under these two rival leaders—Chiang and Mao—were two rival parties. The KMT was corrupt and inefficient, a fact that the democratic façade of the National Assembly of 1946 and 1948, the multi-party Cabinet of 1947, and the Presidential Election of 1948 could not conceal. General [A.C.] Wedemeyer in his report dated 19 September 1947 spoke of the KMT 'whose reactionary leadership, repression, and corruption have caused a loss of popular faith in the Government'. Dr. Leighton Stuart, the U.S. Ambassador, regretted the fact that none of the innumerable reform plans adopted by the KMT was ever carried out. Stuart also commented on the incredible stupidity of the KMT propaganda and traced the origins of the weaknesses of the party:

> And yet this party almost from the time it came into power had tolerated among its officials of all grades graft and greed, idleness and inefficiency, nepotism and factional rivalries—all the evils in short of the corrupt bureaucracy it had overthrown. These evils had become more pronounced after the V-J [Victory over Japan . . .] Day in the attempts to crush communism by a combination of military strength and secret police. . . .

The CCP fared differently in the civil war years. Its membership soared from 1,210,000 at the time of the seventh national congress in April 1945 to 2,500,000 in 1948, 3,000,000 in September 1948, and 4,500,000 at the time of its assumption of national power in 1949. Thus in twelve years it had increased 112 times. Most of the new recruits were peasants. At the seventh congress Mao was elected to the chairmanship not only of the Central Politburo but concurrently of the Central Secretariat, thus combining even greater powers in his hands. The next step in the CCP development came in September 1948 when the Politburo held an enlarged session attended by the 7 regular members, 14 members and alternate members of the Central Committee, 10 high-ranking cadres of various regions, and military commanders, to make decisions on (1) the unification of the administrative system of the 'liberated areas', obviously as a preparatory step towards the establishment of a national government; (2) the training of 30 to 40 thousand cadres for working in urban districts, so that the party's power could be transferred from the countryside to the cities; and (3) the reorganization of the PLA in order to be able to fight positional warfare. . . .

PEOPLE'S LIBERATION ARMY

The PLA grew from strength to strength as the war wore on. At the end of 1945 Mao ordered a halt in the expansion of the communist army in order to intensify training. Despite this, in July 1946 when China was irrevocably committed to civil war, he estimated the total strength of the PLA at 1,278,000, showing an increase of over 400,000 from the end of the Resistance War. This, however, is not as important as the reorganization of the PLA. The idea of organizing field armies was mooted by Mao as early as 1938 in his famous dissertation *On the Protracted War* and the actual reorganization was prepared for in 1945 and carried out in November 1948 when the PLA occupied areas were divided into the northwest, the central, the east, and the north-east and placed under the control of four Field Armies—the 1st led by P'eng Te-huai and Ho Lung, the 2nd by Liu Po-ch'eng and Teng Hsiao-p'ing, the 3rd by Ch'en Yi and Su Yü, and the 4th by Lin Piao and Lo Jung-huan. Soon after the reorganization Mao made his historic announcement that the PLA had achieved numerical superiority over the KMT army, and he went on to say:

> This is a sign that the victory of the Chinese revolution and the realization of peace in China are at hand.

The soldiers of the PLA were well-disciplined and well behaved. Dr. Leighton Stuart praised their morale as being 'excellent', and in Nanking he found:

> In painful contrast [to the KMT] the Communist Party was free from private graft, officers and men lived very much together, simply and identically. . . . There was almost no mal-

treatment of the populace. They borrowed extensively but generally returned these articles or made restitutions. . . .

The exemplary role played by the CCP members among the soldiers, by reminding them of the Three Main Rules of Discipline and the Eight Points for Attention, and the intensification of discipline at the beginning of 1948 when ordinary soldiers were encouraged to air their grievances against their officers and were thoroughly interrogated regarding their class background, work, and fighting spirit, were factors undoubtedly responsible for the soldiers' good conduct.

The war of 1945–9, which was admittedly the continuation of the undecided contest of the 1930s, was waged under vastly different conditions, notably the enormously increased military strength of the CCP; but Mao at the beginning did not make any drastic change in his strategy. From his point of view, it was to be a protracted war of attrition in which,

> It [our policy] should rest on our own strength, and that means regeneration through one's own efforts. . . . Relying on the forces we ourselves organize, we can defeat all Chinese and foreign reactionaries.

In other words, the guiding principle of his strategy was still the preservation of the strength of the PLA rather than dogged disputes over the control of a piece of land or a city. A corollary to this was the sapping and destruction of the KMT military strength by fighting, psychological warfare, interrupting the communications, and capturing equipment. In 1946 Mao expected to settle the quarrels between the parties in five years, but according to Robert Payne, he still had doubt in his mind as to their final outcome. . . .

MAO'S WAR STRATEGY

The PLA's aim which persisted throughout the war was the annihilation of the KMT army at the planned rate of 100 brigades per annum. For fulfilling this, the general strategy had a slightly different emphasis from that during the 1930s and the Resistance War, namely, instead of deploying the PLA units in a guerrilla or manoeuvre warfare, they were concentrated on annihilating the KMT armies one by one. In this way they succeeded, according to the communist claims, in destroying 2,640,000 of the KMT troops and capturing 64,000 machine-guns and 14,100 artillery pieces between July 1946 and June 1948; by June 1950 they had destroyed all together 8,070,000 KMT troops and captured

319,000 machine-guns and 54,000 artillery pieces.

All the time Mao conducted the war with caution until 18 January 1948 when he issued this instruction:

> Oppose overestimation of the enemy's strength. For example: fear of U.S. imperialism; fear of carrying the battle into the KMT areas; fear of wiping out the comprador-feudal system, of distributing the land of the landlords and of confiscating bureaucrat-capital; fear of a long-drawn-out war; and so on.

Although he had discarded the mainly defensive strategy early in 1947, positional war was not adopted as the principal form of struggle until the Politburo meeting in September 1948 and a general frontal attack was not ordered until 21 April 1949, when the KMT régime was obviously crumbling. . . .

Throughout the civil war the National Government was haunted by the spectre of inflation, as ferocious as the one which haunted Central Europe in the 1920s. At the end of 1945 the government's gold and dollar reserves stood at U.S. $83 million, but a year later this dwindled to $450 million and another six months later to some $300 million. The main cause of this rapid increase was the military expenditure which at the same time impelled the Government to issue bank-notes for astronomical figures. From 1946 to 1948 the deficit in the Government budget amounted to 70 per cent. of its revenue and was invariably met by issuing new notes. . . .

The unrestrained issue of notes forced the price level to rise at an ever increasing rate. . . .

In 1947 prices leapt up at two-month intervals and settled at a relatively stable level after every fluctuation. The intervals were shortened to one month at the beginning of 1948, then to a week, until finally the rise became continuous. In the second half of 1947 prices increased by 30 per cent. a month and afterwards they doubled, trebled, and in the end quadrupled themselves. . . .

The story of the simpler economy of the 'liberated areas' is itself simpler [compared to Nationalist-controlled areas]. Prices were much more stable, rising, for instance, by about 68 per cent. from January to June 1948 while in the KMT areas they rose by 19.7 times. Each of the 'liberated areas' had its own currency, well managed and circulating only in that area. The unified currency, *jen-min p'iao*, was not introduced until the end of 1948 but showed a remarkable stability in value throughout 1949. The more notable aspect of the

"THE EAST IS RED"

The Cult of Mao was already developing while Communists struggled first against Japanese invaders and later, against Nationalist troops in a civil war that lasted from 1946 to 1949. According to the cult's beliefs, Mao was the savior of China. This view of Mao was standard in the popular war songs of the era. As historian Chang-Tai Hung notes, one song in particular, "The East Is Red," directly refers to Mao as "the people's savior."

Myths and heroic leaders are closely intertwined. A myth uses symbols or images to inspire the audience; and heroes are powerful symbols which occupy a central place in a myth. Of all the hero symbols in the Communist war music, by far the most influential was that of Mao Zedong. Mao created a focus for unity and a vision of the nation's future; he was seen as a beloved leader who offered selfless devotion to a collective cause, protecting not just the livelihood of the people, but the survival of China as a nation. The symbol of Mao was designed to create an emotional bond between the leader and the people and to mobilize the oppressed populace in whose name the Chinese Communist Party acted. The repeated use of that symbol was a key ingredient in the formation of the cult of Mao during the Yan'an years. . . .

Of all the folk tunes adopted for political use, perhaps none was more influential than 'The East Is Red' in building up the cult of Mao. Based on a northern Shaanxi folk song, 'Riding a White Horse' ('Qi baima'), the old tune was adapted into a new song entitled 'Migrant Melody' ('Yimin ge') by the Shaanxi peasant singer Li Youyuan and his nephew Li Zengzheng in 1943. . . .

In the fall of 1945, as the Communists raced northward to Manchuria to take over Japanese garrisons after the enemy's defeat, the songwriters Liu Chi (1921–), Wang Dahua (1919–1946), and others reworked the piece and gave it a new name: 'The East Is Red'. This version began:

> The east is red,
> The sun is rising.
> China has brought forth Mao Zedong.
> He works for the welfare of the people,
> Hu-er-hai-ya,
> He is the people's great savior.

Chang-Tai Hung, "The Politics of Songs: Myths and Symbols in Chinese Communist War Music, 1937–1949," *Modern Asian Studies*, v. 30, part 4, October 1996.

communist economy was the change in the land policy. In November 1945 Mao reaffirmed his policy of reducing land rent, organizing mutual-aid teams, and giving loans to peasants but refraining from confiscating land. The first sign of breaking away from this moderate policy appeared in December 1946 when the Draft Land Law empowered the government of the Shensi-Kansu-Ninghsia Border Region to purchase compulsorily landlords' excess land. But the cautious approach of the Draft Law made clear the government's fear of driving the landlords and wealthy peasants away from the CCP while the outcome of the civil war was still uncertain. Ten months later, as the prospect became much brighter for the communists, the party's land policy became more radical—the land conference, held at P'ingshan in Hopei in Mao's absence, passed the Outline Land Law of China on 13 September, promulgated by Mao on 10 October. The Law terminated the ownership of all landlords (Article 2) and of temples, schools, and other organizations (Article 3) and abolished all the loans contracted before the date of promulgation (Article 4). It stipulated that all peasant bodies were to elect representatives to a committee which would be responsible for carrying out land reform (Article 5). All land in the 'liberated areas' was to be redistributed among the peasants on an egalitarian basis (Article 5). The political significance of this return to a policy advocated by the Comintern as early as 1927 was to win more enthusiastic support from the poor peasants, thereby consolidating the communist ranks in preparation for the eventual establishment of a new régime. . . .

The poor peasants and communists cadres committed leftist mistakes by labelling some who had not engaged in 'feudal exploitation' as landlords or rich peasants, by encroaching upon the industrial and commercial enterprises of landlords and rich peasants, and by beating and killing without discrimination. Therefore the first instruction Mao issued upon his arrival at the Shansi-Suiyüan Border Region from north Shensi was to stop such excesses. His admonition against encroachment on industrial and commercial enterprises in urban areas was of special importance, for by then the communists were in control of some large cities, for instance, Shihchiachuang and Kaifeng, and a correct attitude towards urban properties was urgently needed lest city dwellers should harden their opposition to the communists.

Hence on 1 September 1948 the editorial of the *Tung-pei Jih-pao* (Northeast Daily) exhorted the communist cadres to protect industrial plants and business organizations because they were 'assets of the nation' and 'the crystallisation of the blood and sweat of the labouring people of China'. . . .

MILITARY CAMPAIGNS

The fight for the control over China is in effect a fight for the control over the 'A' formed by the three major railways—the Tientsin–Pukow, Peking–Hankow, and Lunghai—and the cities along them. A threat to any corner of the 'A' is a real threat to the security of the Central Government and the occupation of it offers a good chance of success to an insurgent. For either the attack or defence of the 'A' it is important to take or maintain its periphery—Honan, Shansi, Inner Mongolia, and Manchuria, especially Manchuria because of its agricultural and industrial potentials and its proximity to Russia and Japan. It was precisely on the periphery that the civil war of 1946 and 1947 was fought. When that stage was over, the 'A' was exposed to attack from north and west and in two decisive campaigns—the Peking–Tientsin and the Hsüchow—it fell into the hands of the communists. Thereafter the communist domination of China as a whole was merely a matter of time. . . .

Before Christmas 1947 when the PLA launched its winter offensive in Manchuria, the morale of the 500,000 KMT troops was already very low and their commanders were hopelessly divided. In ninety days Lin Piao [Lin Biao, PLA general] took no less than nineteen towns including the strategic point Ssup'ingchieh, destroyed some 150,000 of the troops, and compressed the KMT holdings to three small enclaves around Mukden, Ch'angch'un, and Chinchow, a mere 1 per cent. of the total area of Manchuria. . . .

The gain of Manchuria gave the PLA 'a strategically secure rear area with a fair industrial base'; the destruction of 470,000 (Chiang admitted 300,000) of the cream of Chiang's troops not only tipped the military balance but also swelled the ranks of Lin Piao's army from 360,000 to nearly 800,000 and freed them from Manchuria to move against the KMT's north flank, thus virtually sealing the fate of the 10 per cent. of the territories north of the Yellow River still under the KMT; the airlift to the untenable city of Ch'angch'un for two months and four days exhausted the Government defence budget for the 1948–9 fiscal year; it was unwise of Chiang to take personal command of a hopeless campaign and the defeat greatly injured his prestige. . . .

Before the Manchurian campaign started, Mao estimated that five years from July 1946 would be required for the overthrow of the KMT régime; at the beginning of the Huai-hai campaign, he forecast the PLA's crossing of the Yangtze in the autumn of 1949; but half-way through the Huai-hai campaign, on 14 November, he made the announcement that the PLA had achieved its numerical superiority to the KMT army. . . .

But some time before that, in October 1947, he began to call Chiang and other leaders of the KMT 'the civil war criminals'. His reply to Chiang's appeal for peace, dated 5 January, was entitled 'On a War Criminal's Suing for Peace', which was a scathing and merciless attack on Chiang and his policies. . . .

MAO'S PEACE TERMS

[In January 1949] Mao announced his peace terms:

(1) Punish the war criminals; (2) Abolish the bogus constitution; (3) Abolish the bogus 'constituted authority'; (4) Reorganize all reactionary troops on democratic principles; (5) Confiscate bureaucrat-capital; (6) Reform the land system; (7) Abrogate treasonable treaties; (8) Convene a political consultative conference without the participation of reactionary elements, and form a democratic coalition government to take over all the powers of the reactionary Nanking Kuomintang government and of its subordinate governments at all levels. . . .

On 21 April [1949] Mao issued his order to the PLA for the countrywide advance. The 2nd and 3rd Field Armies under Liu Poch'eng and Ch'en Yi crossed the Yangtze at three points while the KMT 'grandiose plans for defence crumbled amid political bickering, desertions or betrayals, disorderly retreats.' Nanking fell on 24 April and a month later Shanghai followed. Thenceforth the collapse gained speed. The 1st Field Army of the PLA mopped up the north-west and south-west from 1949 to February 1950, destroying Hu Tsungnan's army in the process; the 2nd Field Army, having taken Chekiang, drove into Kiangsi and Hunan and then swept across Kwangtung to Szechwan; the 3rd Field Army, after the battles of Nanking and Shanghai, moved along the sea coast to Chekiang and Fukien; and the 4th Field Army defeated General Pai Ch'ung-hsi first at Wuhan on 16 May, then at Hengyang on 11 October, and finally in Kwangsi in December. In the eleven months since the Manchurian campaign the PLA had advanced 2,000 miles to end the war on the mainland at the close of 1949.

Amid these triumphant military activities, the new Political Consultative Conference took place in Peking on 9 September. Addressing its preparatory committee on 15 June, Mao had said that only by proclaiming the foundation of the People's Republic of China and electing a democratic coalition government to represent it could 'our great mother land free herself from a semi-colonial and semi-feudal fate and take the road of independence, freedom, peace, unity, strength, and prosperity'; now at the opening session of the Conference he said:

> We have now entered into the community of peace-loving and freedom-loving nations of the world. We shall work with courage and industry to create our own civilisation and happiness and, at the same time, to promote world peace and freedom.

And on 1 October 1949 Mao, the newly elected Chairman of the People's Republic of China, proclaimed the foundation of the republic for which he had incessantly fought for twenty-two years.

CHAPTER 3

MAO AND THE PEOPLE'S REPUBLIC

PEOPLE
WHO MADE
HISTORY

MAO ZEDONG

Unifying and Building a Nation

Henrietta Harrison

When Mao Zedong declared the establishment of the People's Republic of China on October 1, 1949, he was facing a nation that had been in chaos for well over a century. Civil war, intrusions by European powers, republican revolution, regional warlordism, Japanese invasion, and finally a "war of liberation" had torn apart the fabric of Chinese civic life. Mao and the Chinese Communist Party had the great task of unifying China into a single modern nation.

Historian Henrietta Harrison of Britain's University of Leeds discusses some of the ways that the unification was accomplished. National symbols such as a new flag were established. Territory was integrated. Infrastructure in the form of roads, railways, and radio networks was developed. Farmland was distributed to peasants and the educated class underwent "thought reform," and a national language, Mandarin Chinese, was adopted. Harrison also points out that Mao Zedong himself had become a symbol both of the Communist revolution and the unifying of a new nation.

The Chinese Communist Party had originated among the radical modernisers of the early twentieth century. When it came to power it continued the processes of modernisation and state-building that had been begun under the fragmented governments of the republican period. But although the nationalist goals of the government of the new People's Republic of China may have been similar to those of earlier governments, the new state had an unprecedented ability to impose its will. In this situation many of the projects of the republican period, such as the creation of a national transport network and a national language, came to fruition. The Communist Party also continued the equation of nationalism with support for the party, strengthening the politicisation of nationalism that had begun under the Nationalist Party. Since the version of communism that was promoted by the party was highly moralistic, the effect was to create a politicised nationalism that was reminiscent of the culturalism of the late nineteenth century.

A NEW NATION AND A NEW FLAG

By the beginning of 1949 it was already clear that the Nationalist Party was losing the civil war. The Communists had controlled much of the north China countryside since the early 1940s. Now the major cities had begun to fall to their armies and then those same armies crossed the Yangzi River and moved rapidly across southern China. As the Communist troops entered each city ceremonies and parades were rapidly organised to welcome them. In Beijing, which the People's Liberation Army entered in February 1949, there was a procession of thousands of students and workers, many of them holding banners welcoming the army or portraits of Mao Zedong, already established as the Communist Party's preeminent leader. Among the marchers were stilt walkers and folk-dance groups who entertained the onlookers but also reminded them of the party's rural bases. Other groups chanted the eight conditions that Mao had laid down for a Nationalist Party surrender. After the marchers came a huge display of military power: tanks, armoured cars, artillery and soldiers. Such scenes were repeated across the country, marking out the central features of the party's power: popular enthusiasm among both urban and rural groups, a leadership centred on Mao Zedong, and huge military strength.

Eight months later, on 1 October 1949, Mao Zedong stood on the Tiananmen Gate, the entrance to the Forbidden City at the heart of Beijing, and declared to the crowds beneath the establishment of the government of the new People's Republic of China. The square was decorated with the new red five-star flags and printed flags had been distributed along with the newspapers that day. Like the earlier shining-sun flag, the five-star flag was a statement of political as well as national allegiance. A competition had been held to design the new flag, with the requirement that the design must represent both China as a nation and the new 'democratic dictatorship' under the leadership of the Communist Party and the proletariat. Three thousand entries were submitted, and 38 selected by the organising committee. From these Mao Zedong picked the winning design, saying that it represented the idea of rallying round the party, and his choice was then ratified by a vote of the members of the National People's Political Consultative Conference. The bright-red ground representing both revolutionary enthusiasm and the red earth of China contrasted with the sky blue of the Nationalist Party's flags and emblems. In the upper left-hand corner four small stars encircled one larger one, said at the time to represent the Communist Party and the four classes of 'the people': the national bourgeoisie, the petty bourgeoisie, the workers and the peasants. Together the stars represented the idea of the people's democratic dictatorship as required by the competition rubric. . . .

The leaders of the new state stood together on the Tiananmen Gate. They formed a small group, mostly men dressed in the military-style suits popularised by Sun Yatsen [leader of the 1911 republican revolution]. But it was Mao Zedong whose voice was picked up by the microphones as he read out the formal proclamation announcing the establishment of the new government. As he finished he pressed the switch that caused the new national flag to rise slowly up the great flagpole that had been erected in the centre of the square. Then for three hours the artillery, tanks, cavalry, infantry and military bands of the People's Liberation Army paraded past the leaders, while the spectators marvelled at the smartness of their uniforms, their leather boots, and the quality of their weapons. Aeroplanes flew overhead scattering leaflets. By the time the military review had been completed it was getting dark and the huge procession of political parties, government organisations and others that followed was lit by lanterns. As the marchers passed the reviewing stand they shouted 'Long live the People's Republic' and 'Long live Chairman Mao!' and Mao replied 'Long life to you, comrades!' In many ways the occasion was similar to the National Day ceremonies of the 1920s and 1930s, except that the older symbols of the nation were now replaced by the symbols of the Communist Party, and above all by the figure of Mao Zedong. During the late 1960s and early 1970s Mao was to become a pervasive symbol of both the revolution and the nation: badges, portraits and statues of Mao were omnipresent and it was claimed that love of Mao was the same as love of China. This was foreshadowed on that first evening of the new state, when a huge portrait of Mao hung on the front of the Tiananmen Gate and was illuminated after dark, while Mao's head had replaced that of Sun Yatsen on postage stamps. Again the symbols of the politicised nation were focused on a single man, but now that man was the living leader of the dominant political party. . . .

NATIONAL UNIFICATION

The territory of the new People's Republic of China was basically the same as that which the Nationalist government had laid claim to in the 1930s: the nineteenth-century Manchu empire except for Taiwan and Mongolia. The island of Taiwan had been ceded to the Japanese in 1895 and handed back to China after Japan's defeat in World War II. In 1949, Chiang Kaishek's Nationalist government retreated to the island, and, after the outbreak of the Korean War in 1950, the island was protected from a communist invasion by the United States navy. Taiwan was thus inaccessible to Communist rule, though both the People's Republic and the Nationalist government on the island agreed that it was rightfully part of China. Mongolia, on the other hand, was now recognised by China as an independent state. A Mongol state had been declared in northern Mongolia at the time of the 1911 Revolution and in the 1920s fighting between Russian forces in central Asia had left northern Mongolia as a satellite of the new Soviet Russian state. The alliance between the Chinese Communist Party and the Soviet Union at the time of the formation of the People's Republic meant that the new government was willing to give up China's claim to northern Mongolia. With these two exceptions, the territorial claims of the People's Republic were the same as those of the Nationalist government.

The crucial difference between the rules of the Nationalist and Communist governments lay in the fact that by the end of the 1950s the People's Republic had succeeded in imposing a unified administration on all the areas to which it laid claim. With the arrival of the Communist government, provinces and regions that had been effectively independent since the early 1910s were incorporated into a centrally administered state. Policies made in Beijing were implemented from Liaoning to Yunnan and the central government could transfer its own personnel to any part of the country. This administrative unification was mirrored in the establishment of a rail and road network. Yan Xishan's building of narrow-gauge railway lines in Shanxi province (when the rest of the country used a wider gauge) had been symbolic of the way in which warlord power had divided China during the Republic. Now, not only were the rail links that had been destroyed in the war rebuilt, but the government embarked on a major program of new construction.

ROADS, RAILROADS, AND RADIO

The motives for this construction were strategic and economic, with the rail line out into northwest China providing access to the oil fields of Xinjiang and the lines to Fuzhou and Xiamen allowing the movement of troops to the frontier with the Nationalists on Taiwan. However, the new road and rail links also greatly increased the central government's access to the outlying provinces. Thus the new railway through Sichuan to the provincial capital, Chengdu, limited the province's long-standing autonomy and regionalism. Even more dramatic was the situation in Tibet, where roads were built for the first time linking the capital, Lhasa, to the Chinese provinces of Sichuan in the east, Qinghai in the north and Xinjiang in the west. In addition to road and railway construction, a radio network was set up across the country and local county or township governments were required to assign someone to copy down news specially broadcast at dictation speed. Thus not only could government troops and personnel be rapidly transferred from region to region, but central government policies could reach them immediately wherever they were stationed.

LAND REFORM AND THOUGHT REFORM

The government used this new infrastructure to carry out policies that radically affected people's everyday lives and the organisation of society. State penetration of local society to ensure modernising goals had begun with the late Qing reforms and continued under the Nationalist government, and indeed under regional rulers such as Yan Xishan and Feng Yuxiang. The difference under the People's Republic was not only the radical nature of the policies, something to which earlier governments had sometimes aspired, but the effectiveness of their implementation. Land reform had been carried out in some Communist-held areas during World War II and the civil war, but now it was imposed on rural areas across the country. Land was confiscated from schools, lineages and temples, and redistributed to the poor. Wealthy individuals were labelled landlords and subjected to meetings in which they were accused of exploiting their neighbours and retribution was demanded. Thus, as well as losing their land, they lost the prestige that had been central to their power. Land reform destroyed both the corporate structures of rural society and the power of local elites. Communist activists, who mainly came from poor backgrounds, were placed in positions of power, but remained heavily dependent on the Communist Party and local officials. Thus traditional rural power structures were replaced by a structure that was effectively controlled by the central government. In the cities a series of campaigns in the early 1950s achieved a similar result. These campaigns concentrated on government officials and businessmen to dismantle the network of connections that had linked them together into a structure that had long prevented state control. Officials and businessmen were ordered to attend 'study groups' where they were subjected to considerable pressure to reveal both the connections between them and the various semi-legal or illegal practices that had been used to resist government regulation and taxation. When the businessmen returned to their companies they found their workforce unionised under government control and themselves labelled as capitalists. Again government cadres and party activists formed a new power structure responsive to central government control. A Thought Reform campaign directed at academics and teachers to restrict their teaching to ideas compatible with Marxism demonstrated the power of the state over education. By these means the party was able to take control of local society to a much greater degree than any previous Chinese government.

KOREAN WAR

Intertwined with the campaigns of the early 1950s was the impact of the Korean War. War broke out in 1950 when Communist North Korea launched an attack on South Korea. United Nations, and specifically American, troops supporting South Korea then marched northwards into North Korea and towards the Chinese border. In the face of this threat to its own security, the People's Republic of China sent soldiers as volunteers to assist the North Koreans. The war was portrayed in China as an act of resistance to American imperialism. A campaign urging people to 'Resist America, aid Korea' was launched and people were organised through their work to attend meetings and make donations. Through its soldiers' participation in the war the Communist government was able to reaffirm the link between patriotism and support for the government. The identification of patriotism with support for the government had been central to the politicised nationalism of the republic. In the early 1950s the government not only replaced the power structures of local society, but also began a period when government policies were implemented by campaigns in which the population was mobilised to achieve particular goals. State penetration and the government's claims for patriotic support were increased at the same time.

MANDARIN AS THE NATIONAL LANGUAGE

Administrative unification created an urgent need for a single language of government. Not only did the country now have a unified administration for the first time since the fall of the Qing, but the modern state's demands for greater control over society meant that for the first time a large proportion of the population was expected to need to come into contact with state organisations.

On the occasion of a conference on language reform held in 1955, a government statement explained that a national language was necessary in order to 'increase the political and economic unity of the Han people' and aid socialist construction. This was especially important because the establishment of the new state, with its administrative unification and new communications system, had resulted in many people being transferred around the country. The government posted technical personnel to wherever they were needed, and it was soon obvious that highly trained people found it very hard to operate outside their home areas because of the language barriers. Even in north China, where dialects differed much less than in the south, government employees posted away from their home areas had problems: newly qualified doctors could neither understand nor speak to their patients and education officials could not understand the meetings they attended. Moreover, the institutions of government itself found their operations impeded by language barriers. In Guangdong the provincial People's Congress had to be interpreted into the Cantonese, Hakka and Chaozhou dialects as well as Mandarin. The army too needed a common language. The People's Liberation Army had in practice developed a common language based on the north China dialect and recruits were expected to pick this up after at most a year. However, the army also had to communicate with the local people. One soldier, writing in 1955, reported that his unit had already been stationed in 10 different provinces from the far northeast to Guangdong. Clearly it was impossible for officers and men to learn local dialects if they were transferred as often as this. A common national language was essential to administrative efficiency.

A national language was also seen as a way to increase nationalism. A single language that could be used over the whole country would provide a sense of national unity and counteract traditional regionalism and localism. State officials would no longer need an interpreter in their contacts with local people and this would weaken the power of local officialdom in favour of the central government. Differences in local dialects and regionally based hiring practices meant that it was often difficult for a meeting of all the workers in one factory to understand the same speech. The Guangxi local radio station found it necessary to repeat all its broadcasts in Cantonese and the Liuzhou dialect as well as Mandarin. Moreover, since some dialects varied greatly over very short distances, even this kind of repetition was not always sufficient. On the southeast coast the Wenzhou local radio station claimed that its broadcasts in the Wenzhou dialect could not be understood in places only 50 kilometres from the city. Thus the promotion of a national language was intended to give the state direct access, both through officials and through the media, to the whole population. . . .

During the late 1950s and early 1960s Mandarin was actively promoted by the government. Radio was used to spread the new 'common speech' and Beijing Radio became an informal standard. In order to make its broadcasts more widely understood it omitted some unusual features of the Beijing accent and avoided vocabulary that was only used in the local area. Where more than one pronunciation of a word was current or pronunciations were disputed, letters written to the station by members of the public were used to provide an audience consensus. The outcome was a spoken language that was not only standardised, but was also more accessible to a national audience than the pure Beijing dialect, and thus more acceptable as a national language. Government regulations also required that all People's Liberation Army cultural organisations should use Mandarin and that staff working for national institutions such as the post office or the railway network should study it. Beginning in 1956 all primary schools and teacher-training colleges were required to hold Mandarin classes, and from 1960 they were required to use Mandarin as the language of instruction. The difficulty of implementing such policies is suggested by the fact that the central government issued an identical demand in 2000 and it was still seen as requiring several years to achieve. Nevertheless, most people educated from the 1950s onwards did learn to speak some Mandarin in school even if not all their classes were conducted in Mandarin. . . .

However, the association of Mandarin with the power and prestige of the central government meant that as early as the 1950s it had become necessary for a successful career. This had, in fact, been apparent to many people even before the government began actively to promote Mandarin in 1955. It was reported in Hangzhou, where the first northern cadres to arrive in 1949 needed interpreters, that by 1955 village cadres and activists were using the northern dialect for their meetings. From 1960 some level of Mandarin became virtually mandatory for anyone in a position of responsibility even in country villages: youth leaders, brigade cadres and militia leaders were all required to be able to speak some Mandarin. A natural result of this was an increase in the prestige of Mandarin. This was intensified by the reliance of an increasingly competitive education system on Mandarin, which meant that parents anxious to improve their children's educational chances often encouraged them to speak Mandarin at home.

Improving Public Health

Dominique Hoizey and Marie-Joseph Hoizey

Public health was one of the concerns of the Communist regime under Mao. In this selection from two French scholars, Dominique Hoizey and Marie-Joseph Hoizey, writing on Chinese medicine, Mao calls for a campaign to eliminate pests and improve public hygiene.

Plagues of pests such as rats and flies were largely eradicated in the new China. Infectious and parasitic diseases also were attacked and reduced or eliminated. The campaign against bilharzia, also known as schistosomiasis, was especially effective. To solve this problem, Chinese health officials had to address the problem of contaminated drinking water that is the source of blood flukes, which cause bilharzias. The campaign was so effective that Mao was moved to write a poem, "Farewell to the God of Plagues." Also established were the "barefoot doctors" brigades. Barefoot doctors were peasant farmers who received medical training and provided the first line of care in rural China.

Calling on Communist Party members to be 'promoters of revolution', Mao Zedong during the course of a speech on 9 October 1957 broached the problem of hygiene:

> Then there is the question of eliminating the four pests and paying attention to hygiene. I'm very keen on wiping out the four pests—rats, sparrows, flies and mosquitos. As there are only ten years left, can't we make some preparations and carry out propaganda this year and set about the work next spring? Because that is just the time when flies emerge. I still think that we should wipe out these pests and that the whole nation should pay particular attention to hygiene. This is a question of civilization, the level of which should be significantly raised. There should be an emulation drive; every pos-

Dominique Hoizey and Marie-Joseph Hoizey, *A History of Chinese Medicine*, translated by Paul Bailey. Edinburgh, Scotland: Edinburgh University Press, 1988. Copyright © 1988 by Editions Payot. All rights reserved. Reproduced by permission of the publisher.

sible effort must be made to wipe out these pests and every-one should pay attention to hygiene.

ELIMINATION OF PLAGUES

Given the appalling hygienic conditions under which most Chinese lived, Mao's sense of urgency was understandable. Strict preventive measures were imposed with the aim of eradicating infectious and parasitic diseases. During the 1950s, plague, cholera, smallpox and blackwater fever were gradually eliminated. Measures to combat malaria took a lit-tle longer to succeed, but in 1983 there were no more than 1,360,000 people affected by this disease, a considerable im-provement when one considers that more than 30,000,000 had been affected with it thirty years earlier. With regard to bilharzia, a parasitic disease widespread in China, the Min-ister of Public Health, Cui Yueli, announced in 1986 that it had completely disappeared in 56 of the 348 districts and towns where the disease had raged in 1950. Dr Pierre Rentchnick observed with some validity that in the cam-paign against bilharzia 'the most important aspect was the education of the public, which for the most part whole-heartedly participated in the effort to eradicate from certain regions the snails at the origin of the disease'. Edgar Snow also cites a 1957 report by a British academic, Brian Mae-graith, who emphasised 'the degree of general cooperation obtained from the people'. On 1 July 1958, Mao Zedong, de-lighted by the news that a district in the south had succeeded in eradicating bilharzia, composed a poem entitled 'Farewell to the God of Plagues':

> The waters and hills displayed their green in vain
> When the ablest physicians were baffled by these pests.
> A thousand villages were overrun by brambles and men
>   were feeble;
> Ghosts sang their ballads in a myriad desolate houses.
> Now, in a day, we have leapt around the earth
> And inspected a thousand Milky Ways.
> If the Cowherd asks about the god of plagues,
> Tell him that with joy and sorrow he has been washed
>   away by the tide.

The journal *China Reconstructs* reported in 1985 that in Dali (Yunnan province) 'thirty-two years of effort had re-sulted in halting the progress of bilharzia and saving 235,000 victims'. The report continued that 'as a consequence, out of eleven districts hit by bilharzia, six had virtually been cleared

. . . the tragic scenes of rotting corpses in the household and the living pitifully grieving, houses in a state of collapse and fields being swallowed up by weeds . . . have ended'. In this area, the 'God of Plagues' had been expelled, but only after the most persistent effort: 'Since the end of the 1950s, the inhabitants of Dali, emulating other affected regions, have mobilized their resources in the destruction of the snails'.

DECLINE OF INFECTIOUS DISEASE

In 1986, after thirty-five years of effort to prevent and control leprosy, the number of lepers in China was estimated at 100,000. Thus in the province of Shandong the rate of leprosy fell from 5.07 per 100,000 inhabitants in the years 1955–9 to 0.14 from 1980–4. Throughout the country, more than 10,000 specialists in the disease were trained and over 1,100 leper clinics were opened. A research centre for the control of leprosy was created, while the Chinese Association for the Prevention and Treatment of Leprosy was founded under the direction of Dr Ma Haide. In 1985, an international symposium on leprosy was held in Guangzhou. Finally, research was especially carried out on a plant of the celastraceae family, *Tripterygium wilfordii*, considered 'effective in halting the onset of leprosy'.

During the 1950s, tuberculosis was still a principal cause of death. Anti-TB vaccinations were introduced, and by 1958 17,000,000 had been vaccinated. The mortality rate due to tuberculosis fell from 230 per 100,000 in 1949 to 46 per 100,000 in 1958. Several vaccination campaigns against poliomyelitis were also carried out, and in 1973 Dr Pierre Rentchnick could affirm that 'the People's Republic has equalled the West in the control of poliomyelitis'. Another victory for Chinese medicine was the eradication of venereal disease. One person in particular who played a key role in this campaign was Dr Ma Haide, who directed the Central Institute for Research into Skin and Venereal Diseases. The task was not easy. In 1972, Ma Haide confided to his Swiss colleague, Pierre Rentchnick, that 'as it was not possible to carry out blood tests on the entire population, a way had to be found to track down those carrying the disease, perhaps one out of 100 or 1,000 people'. A questionnaire to reveal hidden cases was tried out first in Hubei, and then in Jiangxi from 1958. The population was mobilised: '3,000 volunteers learned how to carry out blood tests and to vaccinate positive cases with penicillin injections; in two months they tracked down 49,000 suspected cases'.

The Minister of Public Health, Cui Yueli, was pleased to note in 1986 that 'the major cause of death was no longer due to infectious and parasitic diseases but rather to brain haemorrhages, heart problems and malignant tumors'. . . .

This brief overview does not do justice to all the achievements in the medical field since 1949, but some others should be mentioned, such as the first reattachment of a severed hand in 1963 by the pioneer of Chinese microsurgery, Chen Zhongwei. Psychiatry also deserves mention. It has been noted that 'in 1950 the number of beds available in psychiatric wards represented 1.1 per cent of the total number of hospital beds; by 1957 the figure was 3.6 per cent. In 1958 the number of doctors in psychiatric hospitals was sixteen times more than in 1949, while the number of nurses was twenty times more numerous.' Psychiatric facilities expanded considerably from the late 1950s on, and in 1982 a city such as Shanghai had 5,300 beds in various psychiatric establishments compared to 400 before 1949.

Special measures were also taken to ensure the health of elderly people. Geriatric services were provided in all hospitals, while in 1964 the first National Conference on Geriatrics took place in Beijing.

HEALTH INFRASTRUCTURE

The gradual improvement of health conditions in China after 1949 was accompanied by the creation of an infrastructure of health protection. Priority has been given since 1949 to preventive medicine, one of the three objectives adopted by the first National Conference on Public Health held in Beijing on 7 August 1950: all 'health work' *(weisheng gongzuo)* had to be 'aimed at workers, peasants and soldiers' *(mianxiang gong, nong, bing)*, prevention was to be considered 'essential' *(yufang wei zhu)*, and 'Chinese and western medicine were to be combined' *(tuanjie zhongxiyi)*. The most urgent task was to create an appropriate hospital network. In 1952, there were 139,000 beds in public hospitals, an increase of 135 per cent compared to 1951 and 217 per cent compared to 1950. The number of beds exceeded 154,000 in 1953. An indication of the progress made is shown by the fact that in 1981 the country possessed 951,510 hospital beds, that is to say fifteen times more than in 1949 (when the number was 63,767).

These figures concern the important urban centres, but from 1965 the Ministry of Public Health concentrated its efforts on the countryside in line with Mao Zedong's call to 'put the emphasis on health and medical work in the rural areas.' The following personal testimony of a production brigade doctor, as reported by [journalist] Jan Myrdal in his study of a Chinese village in 1969, suggests that such an emphasis had previously been lacking: 'We understood Chairman Mao's call to take power in the domains of medicine and health . . . It was not convenient to see a doctor in town. People had to queue and even then they were not well cared for.' Citing the case of one of his patients, the doctor added that 'he spent thirty entire working days waiting to see a doctor . . . if he needs to be treated again he can now come here.

BAREFOOT DOCTORS

This testimony illustrated the need to establish permanent health care in the countryside. The most innovative measure taken was to train a corps of peasant-physicians capable of treating everyday illnesses. A Chinese doctor explained to [Italian journalist and political figure] Maria-Antonietta Macciocchi in 1970 that 'they do not stop working in the commune, they simply divide their time between medicine and the soil. They are also the living proof that a doctor's work is not totally apart from other people's.' These peasant-physicians were to be known as 'barefoot doctors' and by 1984 totalled 1,280,000 in number. At the same time, an infrastructure of health care was either expanded or created. By the early 1980s, there were 2,829 district hospitals (326,000 beds), 55,000 township hospitals (763,114 beds) and 610,000 dispensaries, in addition to a variety of specialised establishments (to combat epidemics, for example), among which particular mention must be made of health schools because of their role in the training, or perfecting the skills, of barefoot doctors.

University-level medical instruction was adversely affected by the Cultural Revolution, and in 1970 the period of study was reduced from six to three years. Lin Biao [military leader, later rival of Mao] and the Gang of Four [ultra-leftists who led the Cultural Revolution] were later to be accused of destroying medical education (principally with regard to shortening the period of study), 'bringing untold harm to the younger generation'.

Agricultural Communes and the Great Leap Forward

David Curtis Wright

Mao's vision for Chinese agriculture was to forbid privately owned plots and to push all farmers into agricultural collectives. This was tried in the mid-1950s with mixed results, and the cooperatives were subsequently downscaled. Mao, concerned that party officials were departing from his vision of a socialist state, argued forcefully for the reestablishment of the agricultural collectives, and for a new industrialization program. He won the argument, and launched the Great Leap Forward in 1957. Here, University of Calgary historian David Curtis Wright explains that the results were disastrous. The Great Leap Forward led to a famine that left more than 30 million Chinese dead of starvation.

The first decade of the People's Republic started out well enough. The Korean War was a brief but significant interruption to China's plans for domestic reconstruction and political consolidation. Even during the Korean War, however, some reforms proceeded. Positive reforms included the land reform program of confiscating all farmland and redistributing it to landless peasants and reform of marriage law, which outlawed concubinage and polygamy and made it easier for women to obtain divorces. Negative development included a nationwide roundup and execution of more than 500,000 "counterrevolutionaries" (basically anyone deemed hostile to the new Communist regime, including former Nationalist officials and people who had voiced disapproval of what the Communists were doing) and new "reform through

David Curtis Wright, *The History of China*. Westport, CT: Greenwood Press, 2001. Copyright © 2001 by David Curtis Wright. All rights reserved. Reproduced by permission.

labor" techniques that employed backbreaking physical labor and subtle psychological torture. The object of reform-through-labor efforts was to change the thought patterns of people deemed hostile to the new state but not deserving of the death penalty.

AGRICULTURAL COLLECTIVES FORMED

The People's Republic used Soviet models and five-year plans to achieve its socialist transformation. For its first four years, the People's Republic of China, or PRC, focused on education, industrialization, and health care. The first formal Soviet-style-five-year plan, which extended from 1953 to 1957, continued efforts to improve education and health care, but it was concerned primarily with improving heavy industrial and agricultural production. Industrial output steadily increased during this period, thanks largely to the assistance of Soviet industrial experts. Agriculture was, however, a different story. Mao and the more idealistic of the Chinese Communists envisioned an agricultural collectivization scheme under which China's peasants would combine themselves into agricultural producers' cooperatives (often abbreviated APCs) of between 40 and 300 households. These cooperatives would, they anticipated, pool labor and create much more efficient agriculture. In practice, however, the results of collectivization were disappointing, and more practically minded national leaders sought the dissolution of the APCs. The practical camp eventually prevailed over the idealistic camp, and by 1955 several thousand APCs had been disbanded. . . .

For reasons that are not altogether clear, Mao and his critics in the highest levels of the CCP worked out a reconciliation among themselves in the summer of 1957. Perhaps they were fearful of the groundswell of public opinion voiced against them and their party during the abortive Hundred Flowers movement. At any rate, by the summer of 1957, a largely united effort was made by the Chinese Communist Party (CCP) leadership to push forward the agricultural collectivization movement once more. Mao had argued all along that the APC movement had failed in the mid-1950s because it was not pushed *fast* enough. He was impatient to see the agricultural transformation of China through to its completion, and his former critics apparently decided to go along with him and give it one more try.

THE GREAT LEAP FORWARD

The CCP launched the Great Leap Forward in September 1957. Its purposes were twofold: to collectivize agriculture and thereby dramatically increase agricultural production, and to surpass Great Britain in industrial production within the impossibly lofty goal of fifteen years. The collectivization of agriculture was accomplished by October 1958. In industry it was decided that China would follow a decentralized approach, with thousands of small-scale industrial enterprises located throughout the countryside. Huge numbers of peasants were transferred to these local, rural industrial efforts, which led to a shortage of agricultural labor. The results for Chinese agriculture were catastrophic.

Enthusiasm for the Great Leap Forward and its goals was tremendous throughout China. In the countryside a movement against the "four pests" (flies, rats, sparrows, and mosquitoes) was launched, and so many sparrows were killed

MAO'S RESPONSIBILITY FOR THE FAMINE

Local officials around China, under pressure from Mao to succeed at agricultural collectivization, filed false reports that greatly inflated harvest results. When it came time to collect the grain in the Xinyang district of Henan Province, there was no grain to collect. Communist officials blamed the peasants for hoarding. In fact, the peasants were starving. The famine became so bad in Xinyang, and other locations in China, that people were forced to eat grass, tree bark, and in some cases, the dead bodies of their neighbors and family members. Mao refused to believe the reports of famine because it would mean an admission that his policies had failed. He did nothing until the mass starvation was indisputable. Finally, the army was sent to deliver grain. As Jasper Becker, author of Hungry Ghosts: Mao's Secret Famine, *notes, for more than 30 million Chinese who starved, the food relief came too late.*

Ultimately, responsibility for what happened in Henan in 1958–61 rested with Mao himself. He had personally sanctioned the orgy of violence [against peasants who were falsely accused and beaten for hoarding grain] and had held up Xinyang as a model for the rest of the country. As early as the beginning of 1959, Mao had received letters from peasants in some counties in Henan protesting that people were starving to death. He disregarded them and in response to complaints that

that the numbers of insects actually *increased* because the sparrows, their natural predators, were disappearing. With the boundless enthusiasm prevailing in the countryside and the completion of agricultural collectivization, elevated agricultural production goals were announced in the summer of 1958, and bumper crops were expected. Peasants and agricultural leaders naively believed that these impossibly high goals were actually achievable. Government propaganda was at its shrillest pitch in the fall of 1958, and one famous report claimed that peasants at one APC had successfully planted grain so closely and densely together that children could stand on top of the planted stocks and not sink down to the ground.

In industry, the most well-known efforts were the so-called backyard furnaces or small-scale steelmaking efforts that had sprung up all over the countryside by the fall of 1958. Almost 100 million people were diverted for labor in these efforts, and in their enthusiasm to achieve elevated

production team leaders were brutally beating peasants who refused to hand over their hidden grain, he addressed a meeting of provincial leaders in February 1959 as follows: 'We should protect the enthusiasm of cadres and working-class people. As for those 5 per cent of cadres who break the law, we should look at them individually, and help them to overcome their mistakes. If we exaggerate this problem it is not good.' Officials were effectively given *carte blanche* to take any measures they wished to seize the fictitious hoards of grain. . . .

For the entire summer of 1960 Mao did nothing, although it was by then becoming clear even to him that China was starving. The rest of the Chinese leadership was paralysed, waiting for Mao to change his mind. At the beginning of the winter, inspection teams led by senior Party leaders set out from Beijing to gather evidence of what was going on in the countryside. . . .

Whatever the truth of the matter, the famine was broken in early 1961 when about 30,000 men from the People's Liberation Army (PLA) were ordered to occupy Xinyang, distribute the grain in the state granaries and arrest the prefecture's leadership. The army stayed for three or four months. One source said that in Huang Chuan county, people were so weak they could only crawl across the ground to get to the grain. Some died only feet away from it.

Jasper Becker, *Hungry Ghosts: Mao's Secret Famine.* New York: The Free Press, 1996.

production quotas, millions of ordinary Chinese even do-
nated their pots and other metal tools to be melted down.
The results were catastrophic; the steel produced was of inferior, unusable quality, and millions of peasants had been
distracted from their agricultural work, naively believing
that agricultural collectivization would somehow make up
for the absence of their labor.

The autumn harvest of 1958 was disastrously small, but
government propaganda reported that agricultural production had doubled. (The vast majority of the APCs did not
want to disappoint the government with accurate production
reports, so they grossly exaggerated them.) The government
took these inflated production figures at face value and collected grain tax according to them. As a result, millions of
people in China starved to death during the winter of
1958–1959 before the government could get food to them. By
early 1959 there was grain rationing in the cities, and meat
all but disappeared from the markets because farm animals
could not be fed what little grain and other crops had been
produced.

FAILURE AND FAMINE

By the summer of 1959, everyone in China realized that
something had gone disastrously wrong with the Great Leap
Forward, but very few people dared say so openly for fear of
offending Mao and his supporters. One person who did dare
say that the emperor had no clothes was Peng Dehuai, a general with a reputation for bluntness who had been with the
Chinese Communists since the Long March days and was a
hero of the Korean War. At a meeting of the Politburo (a small
and powerful core group of high-level leaders within the Chinese Communist party) held in the summer of 1959 in
Lushan, Peng Dehuai circulated a letter that was scathingly
critical of Mao's policies and the disastrous results of the
Great Leap Forward. Mao was offended at the tone and content of the letter and was aghast to learn that Peng had probably circulated it at the suggestion of Soviet leader Nikita
Khrushchev. Peng's blunt criticisms forced Mao to own up to
the errors of the Great Leap Forward, but Mao excused himself for them with the banal observation that everyone makes
mistakes. He then moved with a vengeance against Peng Dehuai and denounced him as a traitor to China who had done
a foreigner's bidding. Seeing which way the wind was blow-

ing, Peng's supporters (including Deng Xiaoping) abandoned him, and he alone took the fall for his impolitic criticisms of Mao. Peng, who was dismissed as Minister of Defense and replaced by Lin Biao was hounded during the Cultural Revolution over his confrontation with Mao and eventually died in a prison of cruel neglect in 1974. Today, however, Peng's reputation has been posthumously rehabilitated, and he is admired even in Taiwan for his courageous and forthright criticisms of Mao's policies.

The Great Leap Forward was, in reality, a great leap backward. An estimated 20 to 40 million people died of starvation between 1959 and 1962 because of the food shortages created by the movement. (This number, already appallingly tragic enough, would have been much higher had not Canada and Australia sold, over Washington's objections, thousands of tons of wheat to China.) Agricultural production in China did not recover its 1957 levels until the early 1970s. The Great Leap scandalized the Soviets and solidified their determination to distance themselves from Mao's madcap adventurism. For the Nationalists on Taiwan, it was just one more instance of Chinese Communist tyranny. This time, however, instead of fearing and loathing the Communists, the Nationalists simply laughed at them. Ever since Great Leap days, the idiom "primitive methods for making steel" *(tufa liangang)* has been a part of popular speech in Taiwan as an idiom for doing things in a comically outmoded and inefficient manner.

The Cultural Revolution

Jonathan Spence

The dramatic failure of Mao's Great Leap Forward policies made him an unpopular man in the late 1950s. After all, more than 30 million Chinese people had starved to death in his attempts to collectivize Chinese agriculture. Mao feared that he was losing power. He became deeply suspicious not only of Chinese intellectuals, but also his own Chinese Communist Party (CCP) bureaucracy.

In the following excerpt from his biography of Mao, eminent sinologist Jonathan Spence describes events leading up to the ten years of chaos known as the Cultural Revolution. In this period from 1966 to 1976, Chinese society was thrown into upheaval as those who professed themselves loyal to Maoist principles destroyed all symbols of capitalist decadence left in China. Conservative politicians and scholars as well as suspect CCP members were jailed or executed in an orgy of violence. Spence says that Mao created the environment that made the Cultural Revolution possible and encouraged those extreme radical political factions that were willing to launch it. But eventually even Mao came to be shaken by the violence unleashed during the Cultural Revolution. Spence is professor of history at Yale University, recipient of a Guggenheim and a MacArthur Fellowship, and author of many books on China.

Mao seems to have encouraged his immediate family to lead as ordinary a life as possible and not to take an active part in politics, but he was not so protective of his brothers' families. Mao Yuanxin, for example, the son of Mao's younger brother Mao Zemin (executed in Xinjiang in 1943) was en-

Jonathan Spence, *Mao Zedong*. New York: Viking Penguin, 1999. Copyright © 1999 by Jonathan Spence. Reproduced by permission of the publisher.

rolled in the Harbin Institute of Military Engineering in 1964, and Mao used him as a foil for many of his own ideas. Their exchanges were later published. From Mao's questions to his nephew, we can see that he was feeling out a field for himself, in which the next round of the battle could be fought to his advantage. The fact that there was a definite enemy—the forces of "bourgeois revisionism" inside China determined to undermine the revolution—was already firming up in Mao's mind. These enemies might be found anywhere: in rural production brigades and urban factories, in Party committees and public security departments, and in the ministry of culture and the film industry. They were even among the students in Mao Yuanxin's own institute, listening secretly to overseas radio broadcasts and filling their diaries with subversive material. "They" were also behind the role system of lecturing and the pointless examinations that schools used to judge a person's performance.

Now, at the age of seventy, Mao was clearly obsessed with revolutionary continuity and his belief that the young people like Yuanxin would have to bear the standard forward. Five elements were essential in this succession, Mao told his nephew: one must be a genuine Marxist-Leninist; one must be willing to serve the masses wholeheartedly; one must work with the majority and accept their criticisms, even if the criticisms seemed misplaced at the time; one must be a model of obedient discipline under the strictures of democratic centralism; and one must be modest about oneself, always ready to indulge in self-criticism. Looking at his nephew, Mao added the harsh judgment: "You grew up eating honey, and thus far you have never known suffering. In future, if you do not become a rightist, but rather a centrist, I shall be satisfied. You have never suffered, how can you be a leftist?"

With these last words, Mao had posed a question that was to obsess him and many of China's youth into the early years of the Cultural Revolution. His answer was to be based on the idea that waning leftist revolutionary activism could be regenerated by identifying the enemies correctly, and then using all one's ingenuity in rooting them out and destroying them. Mao had stated in the past that it was necessary to "set fires" every few years to keep the revolution alive. But doing that could also frighten people: "It's certainly not easy to set a fire to burn oneself. I've heard that around this area there were some people who had second thoughts and didn't set a big fire." Mao came to see his mission as partly to set the fire, but also to teach the young to do it for themselves.

MAO'S ALLIES

In this strangely apocalyptic mission, Mao found a loose association of allies. One was the defense minister, Lin Biao, who was willing to lead the People's Liberation Army forward into revolution, via the "little red book" of Mao's thought, which Lin commissioned in 1964 and ordered every soldier to read. A year later Lin Biao ordered the abolition of insignia, Soviet-style uniforms, and other signs of officer status throughout the army, re-creating—at least in Mao's mind—an image of the simpler guerrilla aura of military life with which Mao had so long been associated. A second group of allies consisted of certain intellectuals and cadres, many of them based in Shanghai, who had a strongly leftist orientation and were genuinely dismayed by what they saw as the backward-looking direction of industrial and rural policy. A third was centered on Mao's wife, Jiang Qing, who for twenty years after their marriage in Yan'an had not been active in politics. But in 1956, after returning from her medical trip to the Soviet Union, she began to take a lively interest in the current state of film and theater in China. Gradually she formed a nucleus of fellow believers who sought to reinstill revolutionary attitudes into the cultural world and to root out those revisionist elements that—she agreed with Mao—were lurking everywhere. A fourth ally was Kang Sheng, a revolutionary Shanghai labor organizer and spymaster in the 1920s, later trained in police techniques in the Soviet Union. He had introduced Mao to Jiang Qing in Yan'an, and later became head of the Central Committee's security apparatus and of the Central Party School. Kang Sheng [security chief who carried out Mao's purges of his enemies] had been a pioneer in orchestrating a literary inquisition to prove that rightists were "using novels to promote anti-Party activities."

It was natural for these disparate forces to gradually coalesce, to find novelists, dramatists, historians, and philosophers on whom to pile their criticisms, and to use Shanghai as a base for mass campaigns that could also be coordinated with the army's various cultural departments. Once the apparatus of leftist criticism was in place in the cultural sphere, it could easily be switched to tackle problems of education in schools and universities, the municipal Party committees that were technically in charge of those cultural realms or educational systems, and the individual Party leaders to whom those committees reported. If galvanized from the center, a remarkable force might be generated.

MAO'S HOSTILITY TOWARD INTELLECTUALS

By late 1965 this was exactly what began to happen. Mao was frustrated with the laggardly implementation of revolutionary policies, and genuinely suspicious of his own bureaucracy. He had grown to distrust the head of state, Liu Shaoqi, and to be skeptical about Liu's ability to guide the revolution after Mao. Mao also had grown more hostile to intellectuals as the years went by—perhaps because he knew he would never really be one, not even at the level of his own secretaries, whom he would commission to go to the libraries to track down classical sources for him and help with historical references. Mao knew, too, that scholars of the old school like Deng Tuo, the man he had summarily ousted from the *People's Daily*, had their own erudite circles of friends with whom they pursued leisurely hours of classical connoisseurship, which was scarcely different from the lives they might have enjoyed under the old society. They wrote elegant and amusing essays, which were printed in various literary newspapers, that used allegory and analogy to tease the kind of "commandism" that had been so present in the Great Leap, and indeed in the Communist leadership as a whole. It was surely of such men that Mao was thinking when he wrote: "All wisdom comes from the masses. I've always said that intellectuals are the most lacking in intellect. The intellectuals cock their tails in the air, and they think, 'If I don't rank number one in all the world, then I'm at least number two.'"

Mao did not precisely orchestrate the coming of the Cultural Revolution, but he established an environment that made it possible and helped to set many of the people and issues in place. In November 1965 a new round of polemics appeared in a Shanghai journal, attacking the historian Wu Han, who was the direct subordinate of the powerful Party boss Peng Zhen, controller of a five-man group that was the arbiter of the Beijing cultural realm. Peng Zhen was unprepared to handle the onslaught, though publication of the article in Beijing was blocked by his staff. Seizing on the chance disruption as a good trigger for action, Mao moved swiftly to remove the head of the Central Committee's general office, which controlled the flow of crucial information for senior Party leaders. It must have been an added inducement to Mao that this man was Yang Shangkun, who had ordered the bugging devices planted in Mao's personal train and in the guest houses where he stayed. In Yang's place, Mao appointed the head of the central Beijing garrison, whom he knew to be fiercely loyal.

At the same time, Lin Biao began to replace key personnel at the top of the military, including the current army chief of staff and former minister of security Luo Ruiqing. In March 1966, after months of relentless questioning about his political loyalties and his attitudes toward political indoctrination in the army ranks, as well as a major series of "struggle sessions" with his inquisitors, Luo tried to commit suicide by jumping from a building. Mao's wife, Jiang Qing, joined the fray by briefing army commanders on the bourgeois decadence and corruption in the arts, which led to the publication of a joint "army forum on literature and art work." Mao had already, in a meeting with his secretaries, shared with them his conviction that the works of the historian Wu Han were intended to be defenses of Peng Dehuai in his earlier struggle at Lushan, and he proceeded to deepen the attacks on the Beijing party and cultural establishment. Lin Biao sharpened tension by warning that the "right" was planning a coup against Mao. Security was tightened in the Zhongnanhai residential area. Two men knew, as well as any in China, what all this must portend. They were Deng Tuo, the former editor of *People's Daily*, and Tian Jiaying, Mao's confidential secretary for eighteen years, who had reported negatively on the peasants' feelings about communes. In the last weeks of May, both men committed suicide.

RED GUARDS FORM

Much of this struggle had taken place in secret, or at least in the well-insulated world of the Party hierarchy. But in late May, some Beijing University teachers put up wall posters denouncing the rightists, or "capitalist-roaders," in their campuses and in the cultural bureaucracy; Mao endorsed the posters, and students began to follow suit, with attacks against their own teachers. *People's Daily* editorialized in favor of the dissidents, and the movement spread to other cities in China, and from colleges to high schools. Groups of students began to wear paramilitary uniforms with red arm-bands and to declare themselves Red Guards and defenders of Chairman Mao. Mao himself, who had been watching these events from the security of a guest house in the cele-brated beauty spot of Hangzhou, traveled in July to Wuhan and took a leisurely swim down the Yangtze, which was rap-turously publicized across the nation as proof of the chair-man's energy and fitness.

Returning to Beijing, Mao reconstituted the Politburo Standing Committee, to remove or demote those he had identified as his enemies. As for himself, Mao wrote in a brief editorial comment that appeared in *People's Daily:* "My wish is to join all the comrades of our party to learn from the masses, to continue to be a schoolboy." In August, with the oracular pronouncement that "to rebel is justified," and that it was good "to bombard the headquarters," Mao donned military uniform and from the top of Tiananmen reviewed hundreds of thousands of chanting students, accepting from them a Red Guard armband as evidence of his support. By September, several of the rallies were attended by a million people, who began to flock to Beijing from around China. The students from Beijing, in turn, began to travel the coun-tryside in squads—free train travel was made available to them—to spread the word of what was now called the Cul-tural Revolution.

VIOLENCE OF THE CULTURAL REVOLUTION

The violence of the Cultural Revolution was manifested at two levels. One of these was orchestrated from the political center, which was now controlled by a small group totally loyal to Mao, through what was called "The Central Case Examination Group," chaired by China's premier Zhou En-lai but directly accountable to Mao. In its heyday this group was composed of eleven Party members, including Jiang Qing, Chen Boda, and Kang Sheng. Under this leadership group were three bureaus that were assigned their own cases and worked closely with the Beijing garrison com-mand, the army general staff, and the Ministry of Public Se-curity. They investigated 1,262 "principal cases" and an un-known number of "related case offenders."

The job of the three bureaus was to prove the correctness of "rightist" charges—including being Taiwan or Goumindang spies, or "Khrushchev-type persons"—and to use whatever means were necessary to achieve that goal. Torture, sleep deprivation, round-the-clock group interrogations, withholding of food, and many types of mental and physical pressure were used by the case investigators in virtually all cases their victims were prominent or even once-revered revolutionaries. Peng Dehuai was brought back from Sichuan to face his own group of investigators. Incarcerated in high-security prisons (of which Qincheng was the most terrifyingly notorious), the victims could not write letters home or see family. Letters they wrote to Mao or Zhou Enlai requesting more compassionate treatment were filed away, unread. Only "confessions" were considered a tolerable form of writing.

These political prisoners only encountered the outside "revolutionary masses" at carefully orchestrated occasions. Red Guard groups would use printed forms to apply to "borrow" one of the victims, as long as they were "returned promptly." Red Guard units might have to pay the cost of renting a place for these confrontations, which would then be advertised in advance. Certain "struggle rallies" were postponed in case of rain, and some victims were in such demand that their appearances had to be limited to three denunciations a week. Liu Shaoqi died from these experiences, as did Peng Dehuai. Deng Xiaoping survived, perhaps because Mao only intended to intimidate him, not to destroy him altogether. This system of case investigation was spread systematically to the provinces, and by the end of the Cultural Revolution in 1976 as many as two million cadres had been investigated by these or similar means.

The second level of cultural revolutionary violence was unorchestrated, coursing down its own channels in an only vaguely designated direction, in search of rightists or "feudal remnants," "snakes and monsters," or "people in authority taking the capitalist road." An announcement from the "Beijing Number 26 Middle School Red Guards," dated August 1966, gave the kind of program that was to be followed by countless others. Every street was to have a quotation from Chairman Mao prominently displayed, and loudspeakers at every intersection and in all parks were to broadcast his thought. Every household as well as all trains and buses, bicycles and pedicabs, had to have a picture of Mao on its walls. Ticket takers on trains and buses should all declaim

Mao's thought. Every bookstore had to stock Mao's quotations, and every hand in China had to hold one. No one could wear blue jeans, tight pants, "weird women's outfits," or have "slick hairdos or wear rocket shoes." No perfumes or beauty creams could be used. No one could keep pet fish, cats, or dogs, or raise fighting crickets. No shop could sell classical books. All those identified by the masses as landlords, hooligans, rightists, and capitalists had to wear a plaque identifying themselves as such whenever they went out. The minimum amount of persons in any room could be three—all other space had to be given to the state housing bureaus. Children should criticize their elders, and students their teachers. No one under thirty-five might smoke or drink. Hospital service would be simplified, and "complicated treatment must be abolished"; doctors had to write their prescriptions legibly, and not use English words. All schools and colleges were to combine study with productive labor and farmwork. As a proof of its own transformation, the "Number 26 Middle School" would change its name, effectively immediately, to "The Maoism School."

Victims

The number of victims from the uncoordinated violence of the Cultural Revolution is incalculable, but there were many millions. Some of these were killed, some committed suicide. Some were crippled or scarred emotionally for life. Others were tormented for varying periods of time, for an imprecise number of "crimes," such as having known foreigners, owned foreign books or art objects, indulged in classical studies, been dictatorial teachers, or denigrated Mao or the Party through some chance remark. Children suffered for their parents' or grandparents' deeds, or sought to clear themselves of such charges by exhibiting unusual "revolutionary zeal," which might include trashing their own parents' apartments, beating up their schoolteachers, or going to border areas to "serve the people" and "learn from the masses." Many families destroyed their own art objects, burned or shredded their family photographs, diaries, and letters, all of which might be purloined by roving Red Guards. Many Red Guards units fought each other, sometimes to the death, divided along lines of local allegiance or class background, or by occupation, as in the case of some labor union members, construction workers, even prison wardens.

The tiny figure atop the rostrum at Tiananmen, waving his hand in a slow sideways motion to the chanting sea of red flags and little red books spread out before him as far as the eye could see, had only the faintest inklings of the emotions passing through the minds of the weeping faithful. It was enough that they were there, chanting and with tears in their eyes. It was enough that to them he had become, at last, the "Great Helmsman, great teacher, great leader, and the Red, Red sun in their hearts."

The Cult of Mao

Maurice Meisner

Mao held power not only through his political vision and charismatic personality. He also encouraged a personality cult that grew around him early in his leadership. The cult of Mao was expanded to almost religious levels during the Cultural Revolution. Mao came to be seen by millions as symbolic of the Chinese nation, a quasi-religious figure held in awe and reverence. The deified image of Mao was similar to the way the emperors had been viewed under dynastic rule. In this selection, Maurice Meisner traces the development of the cult among peasants after the Long March in 1934, and follows it to its extravagances during the Cultural Revolution. Meisner is Professor Emeritus at the University of Wisconsin and author of many books and articles on China.

Although the cult of Mao Tse-tung (and the more bizarre rituals it generated) was not to emerge full-blown until the Cultural Revolution of the late 1960s, its origins are to be found in China's rural hinterlands three decades earlier, during a more heroic and legendary time in the history of the Chinese Communist movement. When [journalist] Edgar Snow made his way to the tiny Communist base area in the mountains of northern Shensi province in 1936 to interview Mao Tse-tung—at a time when Mao was best known to the outside world (and to most of the Chinese world) for the $250,000 bounty Chiang K'ai-shek [Nationalist leader] had for his head—Snow discovered that the 43-year-old Mao was already known in the Red areas as a man who led "a charmed life." That perception undoubtedly owed much to the heroic ordeal of the Long March, concluded only a year before. For those few who survived that incredible six-thousand mile trek through the wilderness, and for the many more who were inspired by the story of their survival,

Maurice Meisner, *Marxism, Maoism, and Utopianism: Eight Essays.* Madison: The University of Wisconsin Press, 1982. Copyright © 1982 by The Board of Regents of the University of Wisconsin System. All rights reserved. Reproduced by permission.

there emerged a faith in Mao as the prophet who would lead his devoted followers to the promised land. The Long March was not only the time when Mao achieved political supremacy in the Chinese Communist Party; it was also an experience that lent a sacred character to the revolutionary mission he now led—and led to a belief that Mao was the invincible One who was destined to successfully complete that mission. Indeed, the stories and legends which emerged from the Long March often read like Biblical tales of Moses and the Exodus. And the traditions and beliefs born in the early days of the Yenan era retained their sacred character three decades later, when, during the Cultural Revolution of 1966, youthful Red Guards embarked on their own exhausting "long marches" as testimony to their faith in Mao and in the power of his "thought."

THE CULT AMONG PEASANTS

Yet it was among the peasants living in and around the early Communist base areas, perhaps more than among the veterans of the Long March, that the emerging cult of Mao found its deepest and most significant roots. The Red Army, formally commanded by Chu Teh [Zhu De] was popularly known as the "Mao-Chu army," but in some of the more remote areas of the Chinese countryside "Mao-Chu" was thought to be a single personage who would free the peasants from their oppressors and restore justice in the world. As Party history was rewritten to magnify the revolutionary accomplishments of Mao, and diminish the role of other leaders, the Mao-Chu myth soon became the Mao myth, the savior who promised deliverance from suffering. . . .

The popular cult that had begun to grow around Mao Tsetung during the early days of the Yenan era was soon reinforced by official decrees. The rectification campaign of 1942–44 established Mao's writings as the orthodox ideology of the Chinese Communist Party. Party historians began to rewrite the history of the revolution to place Mao at the center of political events since the May Fourth era. The Seventh Party Congress in 1945 not only solidified Mao's political supremacy but also canonized "The Thought of Mao Tse-tung" as the sole guide for the Party's policies and actions. Indeed, the congress was largely a celebration of Mao's leadership. All speakers at the congress lavished praise on Mao and his thought, but, ironically, no one more ardently than Liu

Shao-ch'i [Liu Shaoqi, Mao's heir who was later purged] who proclaimed Mao "the greatest revolutionary and statesman in Chinese history" and China's "greatest theoretician and scientist," and told the assembled delegates that the main task of the Party was to study the thought of Mao Tsetung. Several years later, in 1949, Liu declared that Mao's thought marked a new and higher stage in the development of a universally valid body of Marxist-Leninist theory, and proclaimed that "the road of Mao Tse-tung" was the revolutionary path to be followed by the peoples of all colonial and semicolonial countries. Liu Shao-ch'i played no small part in fashioning the cult that was to bring about his own political downfall less than two decades later.

The Communist victory of 1949, the confirmation of Mao's prophecy of the triumph of the revolutionary countryside over the conservative cities, naturally served to enhance the Chairman's already enormous personal prestige and power— and to reinforce popular perceptions that he was indeed a "savior" and "the star of salvation." Yet however great his personal power, during the early years of the People's Republic Mao did not use that power to impose his will on the new postrevolutionary Party-State, perhaps because the will of the leader and the policies of the Party largely coincided. To be sure, Mao suffered from no lack of popular and official adulation during the time; few official writings and speeches failed to pay due homage to the wisdom of the Chairman and the greatness of his thought. But this already developing cult of Mao was not employed to break the bureaucratic rules which governed the functioning of the new state. The leader of the revolution, and the institutions that the revolution had produced, seemed to be in harmony.

MAO DEFIES THE PARTY

That seemingly harmonious relationship was shattered in the summer of 1955 when Mao defied the majority of Party leaders by launching, very much on his own initiative, the accelerated drive for agricultural collectivization. His 31 July speech "On the Question of Agricultural Cooperation" was delivered not to the central committee of the Party, where Mao found himself in a minority on agrarian policy at the time, but rather to an informal gathering of provincial Party secretaries who happened to be in Peking for a session of the National People's Congress. Relying on his personal prestige,

Mao bypassed and overruled the Party leadership and appealed to local rural Party cadres and, through them, to the rural masses. It was not until three months later that the Party central committee convened to formally ratify the collectivization campaign, which now was already well under way. The demonstration that a massive social movement involving hundreds of millions of peasants could be initiated by the words of the leader of the Party, and did not require the word of the Party as an institution, was one factor contributing to a new political climate conducive to the further growth of the Mao cult. The lesson was not lost on other Party leaders. As the veteran revolutionary Ch'en Yi caustically remarked at the time, Mao's speech on collectivization "settled the debate [on agrarian policy] of the past three years."

No less significant for the blossoming of the cult was the manner in which Mao perceived the relationship between the Chinese Communist Party and the peasant masses in his July 1955 speech. It was a perception that harkened back to the "Hunan Report" of 1927, the document which had announced the appearance of "Maoism" on the political-ideological scene, and it was accompanied by a revival of much of the populist imagery and spirit of the revolutionary years. In 1927 Mao had found the true sources of revolutionary creativity residing not in the Party but rather in the spontaneous movement of the peasantry. It was not the Party that was to judge the revolutionary capacities of the peasantry but rather it was the actions of the peasants themselves that was to be the criterion to judge the revolutionary sufficiency of the Party. "All revolutionary parties and revolutionary comrades will stand before them [the peasants] to be tested, and to be accepted or rejected as they [the peasants] decide," Mao had declared in 1927. In 1955 he once again contrasted a revolutionary peasantry with a party described as insufficiently revolutionary. . . .

THE HUNDRED FLOWERS CAMPAIGN

The tension between the Party and its Chairman intensified during the Hundred Flowers campaign when Mao, determined to break down bureaucratic resistance to the radically new socioeconomic policies he now was advocating, began again to question the revolutionary credentials of the Party. And by doing so, he fostered the political processes which were to make him more than simply the Chairman of the Party. Indeed, the crucial ideological rationale for the leadership cult, which was soon to blossom, was set forth by Mao himself in the most celebrated theoretical treatise of the time—the speech "On the Correct Handling of Contradictions Among the People." Delivered at a non-Party forum in February 1957, Mao enumerated many contradictions in Chinese society, but among them he emphasized the contradiction between "the leadership and the led," between the Party and "the people." In pursuing the matter, Mao suggested that responsibility for the contradiction rested more with the leaders of the Party than with the people they led, and further suggested that on certain issues Party leaders might be wrong and the people might be right. And if the Party was thus not ideologically infallible, as its Chairman now implied, it was therefore permissible and indeed desirable for "the people" to criticize the Party from without—and for Party members to learn from criticisms and views which came from outside their ranks.

The argument had profound implications for the relationship between the leader and the institution over which he presided. For if the people were now free to criticize a party which may have gone ideologically and politically astray, then who was ultimately to speak for "the people" if not Mao himself? Mao, after all, was not merely the Chairman of the Communist Party and Chairman of the People's Republic, but also, and more importantly, he was the acknowledged and celebrated leader of the people's revolution—and thereby possessed special bonds to the masses no one else could claim. If "the people" were to speak, then clearly it was Mao who was their preeminent spokesman. Mao was thus freed from the Leninist discipline of the Party and free to criticize the institution from without in his unique and transcendent role as the representative of the will and wisdom of "the people."

THE GREAT LEAP FORWARD

That was precisely the role Mao assumed in launching the Great Leap Forward campaign in 1958. During the rural communization movement, which aroused chiliastic expectations of the more or less immediate advent of a communist utopia, Mao appeared on the new historical stage in the guise of a utopian prophet who promised to lead those who followed his teachings and instructions to a classless and stateless society. Through direct and visionary appeals to the masses, Mao ignored and bypassed regular bureaucratic channels and established state and Party procedures—and, for a time, forged a direct bond between himself and the peasant masses, a bond between his own utopian visions and popular aspirations for social change and economic abundance. The chiliastic character of the early phase of the mass movement in the countryside was accompanied by an unprecedented glorification of both the person and thought of Mao Tse-tung.

Mao himself did not object to his deification and the semi-sacred aura that had come to surround the position of supreme leadership he had assumed. Indeed, he personally promoted the process. At the beginning of the Great Leap, he provided a quasi-ideological rationale for personality cults by distinguishing between good and bad varieties. . . .

REVERENCE FOR MAO DECLINES

Reverence for Mao Tse-tung declined as the Great Leap campaign faltered, and the bond between Mao and the masses was undermined as the movement disintegrated into organizational chaos and economic crisis. Confronted with what was becoming an increasingly desperate struggle for sheer physical and national survival, utopian hopes faded, the hungry masses turned politically apathetic, and regular Party and state bureaucracies reestablished their authority. During the "bitter years" of 1960–62, Mao yielded the center of the political stage to those who wielded power in his name but ignored his policies and paid only ideological lip service to his "thoughts." It was a time when the Chairman was treated as "a dead ancestor," as he later complained. And it was a situation which created both a political and psychological need to refashion and revive the cult.

THE CULT AND THE CULTURAL REVOLUTION

The process of cult-building which took place in the years immediately preceding the Cultural Revolution was markedly different in character than the previous manifestations of the phenomenon. Hitherto, the cult of Mao had been identified with the heroism of the revolutionary years and the radicalism of mass movements launched in the postrevolutionary era. It had grown in at least a partly spontaneous manner during the course of a distinctively Maoist revolutionary history that spanned the period from the heroics of the Long March to the utopianism of the Great Leap Forward campaign. In the early 1960s, by contrast, the rebuilding of the cult was undertaken at a time when a conservative Party and routinized state apparatus ruled a politically quiescent population. The cult of Mao was now a patently manufactured product, deliberately contrived for immediate political ends. And, incongruously, the task of fabricating it fell largely to the People's Liberation Army, the most bureaucratic and hierarchical agency of the state apparatus, but the one which provided Mao with his main political base at the time and the only institution he regarded as still uncorrupted by "revisionist" ideology. It was the Political Department of the Army that published the first edition of *Quotations from Chairman Mao* in May of 1964, and then proceeded to print almost a billion copies of "the little red book" over the following three years, along with 150 million copies of *The Selected Works of Mao Tse-tung*. . . .

In a January 1965 interview with Snow, Mao candidly acknowledged the existence of the cult, and indeed acknowledged that he regarded personality cults as political assets, suggesting that Nikita Khrushchev's fall from power (which had occurred three months earlier) might well be attributed to the fact that Khrushchev "had no cult of personality at all."

If the cult of Mao fashioned in the early 1960s was a contrived phenomenon, the events of the latter half of that decade dramatically demonstrated that its seemingly artificial character in no way diminished its political potency. Personality cults, if they are to be historically significant, demand cult-worshippers—and the launching of the Cultural Revolution soon revealed that China was a land seething with discontented people longing to worship both the person and "thought" of Mao, and eager to vow loyalty to the now deified Chairman. When Mao issued the Cultural Revolutionary call for the masses to "dare to rebel" against the established authority of the Party and its organizations, tens of millions mobilized (or were mobilized) to do battle in what was described, in the typically chiliastic utopian terms of the time, as a "life and death" struggle to determine whether the revolution would survive to realize its socialist mission or degenerate into a "bourgeois restoration," and succumb to "ghosts, monsters, and demons," the deathly forces of counterrevolution. And in the course of the titanic and chaotic conflicts which ensued, Mao loomed larger than ever before as utopian prophet and supreme leader, directly linked to the "revolutionary masses" through his "thoughts" and his "vision," issuing "instructions" and "directives," which millions of faithful followers translated into new (and often bizarre) forms of revolutionary action.

YOUTH AND THE CULT OF MAO

The earliest and most ardent cult-worshippers of the Cultural Revolution were the youth of China, who viewed Mao as the sole repository of the purity of a romanticized revolutionary past and the prophet who promised to cleanse the corruptions of the present and create a radically new and better future. Those "courageous and daring pathbreakers," as Mao christened the Red Guards, travelled over the land in an iconoclastic crusade against the "four olds," carrying copies of "the little red book" (to which they often attributed semimagical properties), and issued manifestoes proclaiming that "supernatural powers" were to be derived from "Mao Tse-tung's great invincible thought." Political legitimacy was conferred on their sometimes dubious exploits on 18 August 1966, in one of the more chiliastic moments of the Cultural Revolution. Hundreds of thousands of Red Guards gathered in the square beneath the Gate of Heavenly Peace ecstatically awaiting the presence of Mao, who finally appeared at sunrise atop the gate in godlike fashion and donned a red armband to become "Supreme Commander" of the Red Guards.

The prominence of young people in the early phases of the Cultural Revolution conveyed the themes of revolutionary revivalism and rebirth which the cult of Mao symbolized and promoted. Had the movement which proceeded under the aegis of the cult remained a youth crusade, perhaps it might have proved little more than a somewhat exotic episode for sociological investigation. But the movement spread rapidly to encompass other social groups, and soon it became apparent that Mao-worshippers were to be found throughout Chinese society. By the latter months of 1966, the urban proletariat, China's most modern social class and a presumably secular one, responded to the Maoist call to rebel against the Communist Party and its organizations. The multitude of working-class organizations which appeared so massively and rapidly on the new Cultural Revolutionary political stage expressed a diversity of social grievances and economic interests, but all proclaimed total loyalty to Mao, professed faith in his teachings, and performed the rituals of his cult. And although the peasantry was only marginally involved in the battles of the Cultural Revolution, the Mao cult spread throughout the countryside as well. Villages constructed communal "rooms of loyalty" dedicated to Mao's thought, individual peasant households often had their own "tablets of loyalty" where family members gathered in mornings and evenings to pay reverence to the Chairman, and it became customary to recite sayings from "the little red book" before meals. The cult was so all-pervasive that even Mao's most formidable foes were forced to march (if they were to do any political marching at all) under Mao's banners and slogans. As [American journalist] Edgar Snow suggested: "In one sense the whole struggle (of the Cultural Revolution) was over control of the cult and by whom and above all 'for whom' the cult was to be utilized."

One of the most striking features of the cult in its Cultural Revolution manifestations was its infusion with traditional religious symbolism. Just as Chinese emperors of old were "Sons of Heaven" whose virtue linked the social order with the cosmic order, so "Heaven" became the symbol of Mao and he was identified with the forces of the cosmos. In an uneasy fusion of traditional Chinese and modern revolutionary symbolism, the "Mao-sun" was hailed as "the reddest of all suns" whose radiance dwelt in the hearts of all true revolutionaries. Drawing on the imagery of Taoist mysticism, the "thoughts of Mao" were said to be a "magic weapon" that would vanquish his foes, while the foes themselves were condemned in demonic Buddhist terminology as hellish "monsters," "demons," "cow-ghosts," and "snake-gods". Exhibition halls commemorating Mao's revolutionary deeds were built across the land, their halls facing east to the source of light, their floors laid in traditional-style mosaics decorated with sunflowers. The official press referred to these halls as "sacred shrines," and peasants who paid reverence to Mao before their "tablets of loyalty" did so much in the same fashion as they traditionally venerated ancestral tablets. . . .

EXTRAVAGANCE OF THE CULT

As the fervors of the Cultural Revolution waned in 1968, and as Mao Tse-tung increasingly moderated the radical thrust of the mass movement he had called into being, the cult of the

Chairman, ironically, grew ever more extravagant. Mao's writings were printed and distributed in ever greater numbers, to the exclusion of virtually all other writings. His portraits, statues, and plaster busts grew both in size and volume. But whereas in the early days of the Cultural Revolution the cult had been identified with a genuine and largely spontaneous mass revolutionary movement, it now manifested itself more in the performance of the established rituals of an orthodox church. In Peking, in the summer of 1968, observers noted "a grimness reflected in the faces of a people who still marched behind crimson banners and portraits of the Chairman, but who did so out of habit." And it was reported that "PLA teams fostered group therapy sessions all over Peking, at which members of opposing factions sat together and embroidered portraits of the Chairman." Schoolchildren, rather than saying "good morning," began the day by chanting "May Chairman Mao live ten thousand years ten thousand times," which, it was boasted at the time, were the first words taught children attending schools for the deaf. Increasingly massive numbers of people came on organized pilgrimages to pay homage at the "sacred shrines" built to commemorate the life of Mao Tse-tung. The test of loyalty to Mao came to be measured less by revolutionary acts inspired by his "thought" than by the ability to memorize his maxims and sayings, and by the size of his portraits carried in the streets and hung in homes. At the beginning of the Cultural Revolution, the Mao cult had stimulated the masses to take revolutionary and iconoclastic actions; at the end of the upheaval it simply produced icons for the masses to worship....

In the end, the Cultural Revolution failed to yield viable political institutions to take the place of the Chinese Communist Party, and Mao was forced to reestablish the authority of the Party in its old Leninist and pre-Cultural Revolution form, although now with the Chairman as its real as well as titular head. The cult of Mao, or more precisely, its more extreme and irrational aspects, were discarded in direct proportion to the process of Party rebuilding in the early 1970s.

CHAPTER 4

AFTER MAO

MAO ZEDONG

The Transition from Mao Zedong to Deng Xiaoping

Edward J. Lazzerini

After Mao's death in 1976, there was a shift in power and by 1979, Deng Xiaoping (1904–1997) had emerged as the new leader of China. Deng set the nation on a new road by supporting the Four Modernizations of agriculture, industry, national defense, and technology. He also shed some of Mao's anti-capitalist rhetoric, informing the Chinese people that "to get rich is glorious." These were economic goals with a very different vision than Mao Zedong's vision. In this selection from his book on the Chinese Communist revolution, University of New Orleans professor Edward J. Lazzerini compares the ideologies, thought, and even the personality cults of China's two great leaders of the twentieth century: Mao Zedong and Deng Xiaoping.

Of those who helped shape the Chinese Revolution over its hundred-year history, few have had the kind of influence as had Deng Xiaoping. Next to Mao Zedong, Deng likely will be remembered as the Revolution's most pivotal figure, particularly in its late twentieth-century phase. Deng was remarkably successful in weathering the vagaries of decades of political struggle within the Chinese Communist Party (CCP) and he outlived Mao to become the man most responsible for reversing the direction of China's development that had dominated until Mao's death in 1976. Deng proved to be a consummate politician, adept at forging networks of relationships with important and useful people (including Mao and [Premier] Zhou Enlai), but his political skills were increasingly associated with reform that has transformed China since the late 1970s by means that Mao long struggled

Edward J. Lazzerini, *The Chinese Revolution.* Westport, CT: Greenwood Press, 1999. Copyright © 1999 by Edward J. Lazzerini. Reproduced by permission.

against. China's Revolution, then, is in significant ways a reflection of the tension between Mao and Deng over theory and practice (work style), despite the extremely close, supportive, and trusting relationship between the two men for most of the decades since the mid-1930s.

MAO VERSUS DENG

The basic features of Deng Xiaoping's thought, canonized in the early 1990s by the CCP's leadership, are distinguished by a pragmatic concern for material results (development before socialism), the forces rather than relations of production, and maintenance of a strong state dominated by a single-party system (the Leninist vanguard party). For Mao, theory (socialism) took precedence over development. This prompted him to pursue policies—as during the Great Leap Forward and the Cultural Revolution—that frequently seemed irrational and proved disastrous to the country's economic well-being. Deng saw socialism as a long-term goal that could be reached only after equally long-term development of China's economic infrastructure and an incremental but persistent rise in the standard of living for the general population. Moreover, Deng typically pushed for more-rapid rather than slower growth in the economy and was willing to accept the negative consequences of such growth—including high levels of inflation and other signs of an overheated economy—that raised concerns in the minds of others, such as Li Peng and Chen Yun.

Two episodes reveal Deng's thinking on this score. Over a five-week period from January 18 to February 21, 1992, Deng made what was termed a "southern tour," visiting Guangzhou, Shanghai, Wuchang, and the special economic zones of Shenzhen and Zhuhai. The tour followed implementation, under Li Peng's direction, of cautious economic policies in place since the autumn of 1988. Impressed by the free-wheeling market practices (capitalism) in Guangzhou, which was in the forefront of such developments, Deng declared that "low-speed development is equal to stagnation or even retrogression" and repeated the principle that the sole criterion for judging the worth of all policies should be economic results. By May 1992 Deng's "southern tour" comments had become the basis of policy, and in October, at the Fourteenth Congress of the CCP, were hailed as a "great theoretical breakthrough." The congress ratified Deng's prescription for "enlivening the economy," thereby substituting a "socialist market economic system" for the Maoist "socialist planned market economy."

In October 1993 Zhu Rongji [China's current prime minister], recently appointed governor of the central People's Bank of China and thereby in control of the country's financial policy, faced the task of reducing inflation in an economy that had become supercharged. He pushed for cutbacks in spending to cool inflation, but his choice of a more moderate pace to development was rejected by Deng, who declared succinctly that "slow growth is not socialism." A subsequent visit to Shanghai in February 1994, which was rapidly surpassing Guangzhou as the country's chief financial center, further affirmed Deng's position and ensured that Zhu's austerity program would be scrapped. The push for rapid growth confirmed Deng's startling dictum that "to get rich is glorious."

MAO ON RELATIONS OF PRODUCTION

Relations of production, linked to a deep concern for class contradictions, antagonisms, and struggle, had figured prominently in Mao's theories of revolution and revolutionary development. Perhaps foremost in Mao's thinking was fear of the consequences of capitalist economics and a desire to avoid introducing any measures that would leave control of the relations of production in the hands of a relative few (capitalists), a not uncommon sentiment among twentieth-century revolutionaries in China and elsewhere. At the heart of this fear was an ethic of egalitarianism that, in its most expansive form, envisioned a society free from social tensions precisely because significant property (land, equipment, finances) would be private no longer.

For Deng, the propertyless society, for all its appeal, was at best distant and left to future generations to witness. In the short and intermediate term, placing property in the hands of as many as possible seemed the best means by which to ensure the personal responsibility required to develop the economy, raise the standard of living, and thereby create the material base for a meaningful socialist society. Deng rejected the notion of the "iron rice bowl" that had promised cradle-to-grave security to China's population regardless of productivity. Instead, he sanctioned the pursuit of profit and tolerated the temporary—it was hoped—material inequities that would result from diminished state control over economic activity. "Some must get rich first," he declared, whether as individuals or regions, or all would remain poor.

The evidence is clear that the fate of the Soviet Union and its eastern European satellites in the late 1980s and early 1990s provided important lessons to Deng. For him, the collapse of the Soviet system resulted primarily from the failure of Mikhail Gorbachev, in his eagerness to reform his country and improve its productive competitiveness, to maintain the reins of politics and authority in the hands of the Communist Party of the Soviet Union (CPSU). By attempting simultaneously to pursue *glasnost* (openness), *demokratiia* (democracy), and *perestroika* (restructuring), Gorbachev succeeded only in dismantling seventy years of institutional and infrastructural development and leaving the country leaderless, directionless, confused, and nearly overwhelmed by economic, political, and social drift that threatened anarchy and civil war. The creation of a parliamentary body and the inexorable movement toward multiparty politics meant more than just the diminution of the CPSU's role. It meant leaving the successor states of the USSR to embark upon a process of transition that produced as many problems as solutions, stalled economic development of many republics even as it enriched individuals, dramatically increased unemployment and underemployment, significantly reduced the standard of living for the majority of people, and pushed the region to the level of less-developed status.

ON PARTY LEADERSHIP

These developments confirmed for Deng what he had long believed: The success of the revolution in China depended primarily on the leading role of the CCP, unchallenged in its "responsibility" to control the commanding heights of authority. In this narrow respect, Deng's thinking was no different from Mao's. Both men had worked together for decades to produce a party organization that could provide just such leadership, but ultimately they differed over the full significance of the party and the principles of organization and bureaucracy. For Mao, excessive organization and bureaucratic work methods threatened to stifle the ultimate goals of the revolution, thereby leading him to embrace the politics of mass mobilization. Going around the party directly to the people, even encouraging actions that might temporarily upset the party's ability to function efficiently and effectively, became hallmarks of Mao's revolutionary method that found expression most fully, but hardly only, during the Great Leap Forward and Cultural Revolution.

For all of his basic loyalty to Mao, Deng sorely distrusted such methods. He criticized them as "leftist excesses" and consistently voiced the contrary viewpoint that placed clear emphasis on the need for a strong party/state. The energy and will of the people, though indisputably important, were only the raw material with which the CCP could work to transform the country. Without organization and discipline consistently and persistently applied, without party rule that was purposeful, focused, and unified, and without a sound program of structured socialization, China's development would be haphazard and fitful in its progress, and the revolution ultimately discredited. To attack the CCP and government as Mao did

---

CHINA'S CONSUMER REVOLUTION

One of the results of Deng Xiaoping's economic reforms was a dramatic increase in the standard of living for the average Chinese citizen. More money translated into more consumer purchases. The consumer revolution is still under way in contemporary China. As Deborah S. Davis asserts in the following selection, the change in economics has led to a change in the individual's relationship to the state as was formerly defined under Maoism.

For China's urban residents, the financial gains from post-Mao economic reform have been rapid and impressive. Adjusted for inflation, per capita income doubled between 1978 and 1990, and between 1990 and 1994 it increased another 50 percent. Savings of urban households rose from $2 billion in 1978 to $63 billion in 1990 and to $192 billion in 1994. Consumer durables such as washing machines and refrigerators that had once been available only to a specially connected minority became routine purchases, and a host of previously exotic products could be found in retail outlets throughout urban China. In 1990 there were 20,000 cellular phones in China; by the mid-1990s that number had risen to 3.4 million. English–Chinese dictionaries once had no official translation for "greeting card," but by 1995 a street stall in Beijing reportedly sold 80,000 cards in one day. Shanghai in 1985 had 52 dance halls and discos; by 1994 it had more than 1,000. In Shenzhen the number of bowling alleys grew by a factor of 40 in one year.

was to foster confusion, undermine the very authority that Deng deemed so vital, and weaken the relationship between party and people. Nothing could substitute for party rule in Deng's mind, as his words and actions repeatedly showed. He led the Anti-Rightist campaign in 1957 because the party's unity was threatened, and thirty-two years later in 1989 he ousted Zhao Ziyang for attempting to split the party during the Tiananmen affair [when the military was used to crush a student revolt]. In between he struggled against the leftists for essentially the same reasons. Even economic modernization, so dear to Deng, would have to give way to the principle of party rule if necessary in the short term.

Over the long term, however, the vanguard role of the CCP was only justified by success in fostering the material development of China. The nexus between party and popular welfare, between the growth of the socialist state and the

When within less than a decade millions of people gained access to advanced modes of communication, new vocabularies of social discourse, and novel forms of leisure through newly commercialized outlets, it does not seem an exaggeration to claim that a revolution in consumption had occurred. Moreover, this rapid commercialization of consumption did more than simply increase consumer choice and raise the material standard of living; it also broke the monopolies that had previously cast urban consumers in the role of supplicants to the state. When party and government officials loosened their control over the flow of commodities, they also ceded greater autonomy to everyday sociability. In granting market principles new legitimacy to coordinate economic transactions, the reforms became increasingly indifferent to the ways in which citizens used their new commercial freedoms. And in this less censored terrain, urban residents initiated networks of trust, reciprocity, and attachment that differed from the vertical relationship and obedience between subject-citizens and party or government officials. The extent to which these investments in unofficial social relationships threaten the political monopolies claimed by the Leninist state remains open to debate and empirical investigation. But although the private has not triumphed over the public, the greater affluence and new consumerism of the 1990s have weakened the hegemonic sureties that defined urban life throughout the 1960s and 1970s.

Deborah S. Davis, "China's Consumer Revolution," *Current History*, vol. 99, issue 638, September, 2000.

development of productive forces and the people's living standards, was from Deng's perspective defining. In a view reminiscent of the obligation that Confucius once placed upon the emperor and his officials, the party could earn and maintain its right to rule only by demonstrating the correctness of its policies through tangible evidence of the people's betterment. Without such betterment why would the people follow the party? On the other hand, the benefits of an economic boom and waves of consumerism, as has occurred in the 1990s, can go a long way toward muffling popular discontent over other matters. Or so Deng and his supporters dared assume.

MAO'S ISOLATIONISM REJECTED

To assist with achieving the economic modernization that Deng believed was at the heart of the revolution and that one day would result in the existence of an egalitarian (socialist) and rich nation, a reversal of Mao's international approach was needed as well. That approach had been decidedly isolationist, much as Joseph Stalin's had been for the Soviet Union until his death in 1953. The reasons behind it are complex but reflect a combination of concerns that were both theoretical—including a deliberate division of global politics between forces of light (revolution) and forces of darkness (capitalism)—and practical—fear of the influences that might arrive from abroad to corrupt or distract the revolution. Deng's "open-door" initiative that dominated the 1980s was designed to bring China more fully into the family of nations, thereby creating opportunities for Chinese students to study abroad and for foreign technology, business practices, and investment to enter China and help further the goals of economic modernization. It is ironic that Deng should have had to resort to this policy, because he was not unconcerned about the negative effects of "bourgeois pollution." But the benefits clearly outweighed the dangers for him, and despite momentary pauses, the policy continued until his death in 1997 and shows no sign of being reduced or reversed by his successors.

For all of his innovations, Deng was in many respects quite conservative. Much like the early Mikhail Gorbachev, he did not proceed from a radical critique of his country's problems but proposed to return to the traditions that he believed had once guided the party and country properly and effectively, as during the mid-1950s and early 1960s. These traditions, drawn from the party's experiences over the decades before 1949, included party democracy (the sharing of authority among leaders, the importance of cadres at all levels, and the practice of the "mass line" that linked party work with popular input), an efficient political system that provided orderly leadership and direction for social development, and economic modernization. These reflected conventional ways of doing things that respected order and discipline while restraining radical experiments. Many of the policies that Deng introduced after 1976 had been conceived much earlier and often by others, only to be set aside time and again by Mao in his pursuit of ideological correctness and his own preeminence.

DENG AND DISSIDENT WEI

In popular lore, both Chinese and foreign, Deng is frequently associated with advocacy of the "four modernizations" (agriculture, industry, national defense, and science and technology). But on December 5, 1978, a young man named Wei Jingsheng put up a "big-character" wall poster in Beijing that he entitled "The Fifth Modernization." Whereas Deng and the party had declared the four modernizations sufficient for transforming China, Wei insisted that a fifth—democracy, popular not party—was even more critical, without which the other four would falter. Rejecting the Leninist notion that democracy would flow from socialism (therefore, the ends justify the means), an idea that helped define the Chinese revolution as well, Wei argued that the achievement of a socialist society required democracy as a condition (in effect, the means justify the ends). Persecuted for his views, Wei has spent many years since 1978 in prison (he was allowed to leave China for the United States in 1997 for "humanitarian" reasons), suffering enormously but remaining unrepentant.

During his prison years, Wei developed the habit of writing letters to Deng Xiaoping (never delivered, apparently), continuing to question and challenge the leader and his policies while identifying some of the most fundamental flaws in the latter's thinking. In Wei's opinion, Deng's most significant error remained his failure to incorporate democratic and human rights principles in either theory or practice. Thereby, argued Wei, the Chinese people were "enslaved" to the dictates of their masters who, like the former emperors, dwell in halls of power to which the people are forbidden.

Deng had critics within the CCP itself, in top leaders such as Li Peng, the Soviet-educated bureaucrat for whom the label "Stalinist" would not be inappropriate, or in Yang Shangkun, one of the party elders linked closely to the military. Their criticisms were generally muted in the face of Deng's authority and the popularity of his policies, but they were not without purpose or consequence. Differences of opinion, debate, and even factionalism in the history of the CCP have been common, at times leading to compromise, at others to the party's purging of "incorrect thought," and still others to serving the larger interests of the preeminent leader, first Mao then Deng. Frequently, Mao and Deng "allowed" their opponents to test alternative policies either to create possibilities for their denunciation or to provide respites to policies in place and likely to continue. Deng, for example, when faced with an inflationary spiral and an overheating economy around 1989, had to entertain measures contrary to his own thinking, but he never intended to establish their permanence. Rather, he used them for the moment before moving on. . . .

THE PERSONALITY CULTS

However much he chastised Mao for succumbing to a "personality cult" that placed him above all others and turned the party into a personal reflection, Deng was prone to fall into the same trap, giving up party, government, and military offices but retaining the authority that comes from being recognized as "paramount leader." After 1989, Deng's own personality cult became more pronounced with the publication of increasing numbers of his speeches, "private" conversations with other party leaders and foreign visitors, and a biography written by his daughter in 1993. In addition, Deng's heir apparent, Jiang Zemin, and others began to speak more frequently of "Deng Xiaoping Thought," thereby raising Deng's ideas to the pinnacle of theoretical respectability and unassailability. This has continued since Deng's death, serving as the basis of the consensus upon which Jiang relies to legitimize his own authority and to sustain the fundamental direction for the country that Deng set.

Political reform for Deng was, at best, very narrowly defined and aimed at little more than making party cadres "better educated, professionally more competent, and younger."

Such goals serve the interests of state efficiency and effectiveness but do little to devolve power to the people. Neither do they dilute the authority of the one party permitted to function. Deng's distaste for democracy manifested itself continually during his life, whether in the crackdown against intellectuals during the Hundred Flowers campaign of 1957, or that against the democracy movement in 1979, 1986, and 1989. This is perhaps understandable of someone so committed to state power, but it leaves China with the question of political modernization unanswered. Signs of further loosening of political restraints under Jiang Zemin are encouraging but tentative and unlikely to do more in the near future than whet the appetites of the relatively small number of democratic advocates.

RECONCEPTION OF SOCIALISM

What may help accelerate changes within the political realm is something that has been happening within the past two decades in China. A subtle and occasionally public debate has been unfolding concerning the merits of socialism as a philosophy of social justice and a program of national development. Thus, accompanying the grand experiment with market-based reforms that has challenged Marxist-Leninist-Maoist dogma on economic policy has been a profound re-examination of China's socialist theory and practice. At its core, this debate centers on the question of whether many of the root problems that China continues to face are the consequence of Chinese socialism in particular and Marxism in general. The direction of policy under Deng and his successor is clear evidence that the debate is leaning to one side. As the American political scientist Yan Sun has argued in an important recent book, the fate of socialism in China and China's future will mean the decline of "ideological monopoly and hence a singular view of social order and development." Both inside the party and outside (especially among intellectuals), a pluralistic conception of socialism has meant a significant moderation of ideological labeling and concern for deviation. Instead, the leadership seems more attentive to doctrinaire and destructive tendencies on the Left (the general position associated with Mao), the "reconceptualization" of socialism, and the search by the public itself for "new solutions to new problems." More than market-based reforms, this may be Deng Xiaoping's most important legacy.

Evaluating the Communist Revolution

Maurice Meisner

While University of Wisconsin Professor Emeritus Maurice Meisner admits that Mao Zedong was responsible for countless atrocities, he also points out that many advances were made in the Mao years as ruler of China. Unifying the nation and forming a central government was no small feat for a nation that had been in upheaval for more than 100 years. Land reform and social reform that gave more options for peasants and women were also positive gains. The industrial development and creation of a national infrastructure developed during Mao's regime would be the basis of the Deng-era economic advances to follow. Even though millions died during the great famine following Mao's failed Great Leap Forward, overall the standard of living improved for the average Chinese person during the Mao years.

It is easy enough today, after a half-century of the Chinese Communist Party in power, to forget that the "long revolution" that produced the People's Republic of China in 1949 was probably the most popular and certainly the most massive revolution in world history. Those who actively participated in and supported the rural-based Maoist-revolution in the 1930s and 1940s did so in numbers unprecedented in the history of revolutionary movements.

The Chinese Communist revolution was also perhaps the most heroic of all revolutions, a heroism symbolized by the legendary Long March of the mid-1930s. But courageous acts were by no means confined to those who embarked on that extraordinary journey, for the revolution's success required enormous sacrifices by tens of millions of people in both cities and villages. The Communist revolution in China

Maurice Meisner, "China's Communist Revolution: A Half-Century Perspective," *Current History*, vol. 98, September 1999, pp. 243–48. Copyright © 1999 by Current History, Inc. Reprinted with permission.

was not a coup d'état carried out by a small group of revolutionary conspirators.

Yet revolutions, in the end, are judged not by the numbers who participated or the degree of their heroism, however fascinating and significant these aspects of the original revolutionary act may have been. Rather, revolutions are historically judged and characterized by their ultimate social and political results. What then are the social results of the Maoist revolution that culminated in the political victory of 1949?. . .

MAO'S ACCOMPLISHMENTS

While Maoist ideology and intentions were often ambiguous, the policies of the Communist regime during the early years of the People's Republic were concrete and the accomplishments quite remarkable. The first, and essential, achievement was the fulfillment of the goals of the ill-fated Kuomintang [Guomindang]-Communist alliance of the mid-1920s. The alliance had been forged to pursue two essential nationalist aims: first, national unity (elimination of warlordism and establishment of an effective central government), and, second, national independence (elimination of the foreign encroachments that had humbled and humiliated China for almost a century). But the Kuomintang-Communist alliance floundered in 1927 because of the popular social radicalism it had unleashed, and the victorious Kuomintang regime of Chiang Kai-shek proved ineffective in pursuing its nationalist mission in the years that followed. Yet these elemental nationalist goals of unity and independence, which had proved elusive for so many decades, were achieved by the Communists in a few months following their victory in 1949.

The establishment of an effective central government was an enormous achievement for a country that for more than a century had suffered from internal political disintegration and external impingement, and all the human suffering these entailed. Moreover, the political achievement was the essential prerequisite for progress in all other areas of social and economic life. Among these, in the early years of the new regime were the revival and reformation of China's vice-ridden cities, fundamental sanitation and health measures, the Marriage Law of 1950 (which proclaimed at least formal legal equality between men and women), and the Land Reform campaign of 1950–1952.

Land reform was an especially important accomplishment. It eliminated China's gentry-landlords, the oldest ruling class in world history and a major impediment to modernization. It brought some measure of socioeconomic equity to the Chinese countryside and cemented the powerful tie between the Chinese Communist Party and the majority of peasants. It joined even the most remote villages to a national political structure by implanting party organizations of young peasant activists in localities throughout the countryside. Furthermore, land reform was the essential precondition for modern industrial development. By removing a parasitic landlord class and by establishing an effective political mechanism to channel the agrarian surplus to finance urban industry, the Communist revolution opened the way for the industrial revolution that transformed China from a predominantly agrarian to a mainly industrial nation within a period of several decades. The relationship between land reform and industrialization was understood by Chinese Communist leaders well before Western modernization theorists came across the insight. . . .

INDUSTRIALIZATION

Modern industrial development duly began in intensive fashion with the Soviet-modeled first five year plan in 1953. What followed over the remainder of the Mao era (to 1976) and, in even more impressive fashion during the era of Deng Xiaoping (1978–1997), undoubtedly will be recorded as the most rapid process of industrialization over a sustained period in history. For nearly half a century, China, long known as "the sick man of Asia" and among the most impoverished lands by any measurement, has experienced an industrial growth rate averaging 10 percent annually. This has resulted in China's emergence today as the world's second-largest industrial producer (after the United States) and as the country with the third-largest GDP (after the United States and Japan) as measured in purchasing power parity.

China's transformation from an agrarian to a primarily industrial nation (in terms of the value of production and probably employment as well) cannot be attributed solely to Deng's market reforms, as is often supposed. The process began under the long rule of Mao, about whose accomplishments many Western scholars have grown strangely silent, fearful that they will be seen as apologists for the crimes of the era should they mention its real accomplishments. Nonetheless, during the Mao period the basic foundations of China's industrial revolution were laid. Without that foundation, the post-Mao reformers would have had little to reform. As distinguished Australian economist Y.Y. Kueh has observed, Maoist China's "sharp rise [30 percent] in industry's share in national income is a rare historical phenomenon. For example, during the first four or five decades of their drive to modern industrialization, the industrial share rose by only 11% in Britain (1801–1841); and 22% in Japan (1882–1927). In the post-war experience of newly industrializing countries, probably only Taiwan has demonstrated as impressive a record as China in this respect."

Costs and Gains

The social, human, and environmental costs of industrialization have been (and remain) high in China, as has been the case with virtually every industrializing country since the early nineteenth century. In China these costs were paid primarily by the peasantry, the most numerous and poorest members of the population. Yet it is difficult to imagine that there might have been a viable alternative. As sociologist Barrington Moore observed in *Social Origins of Dictatorship and Democracy*, "The tragic fact of the matter is that the poor bear the heaviest costs of modernization under both socialist and capitalist auspices. The only justification for imposing the costs is that they would become steadily worse off without it."

During the Mao era the Chinese people as a whole became markedly better-off, even taking into account all the crimes and blunders of the time, among which the famine resulting from the ill-fated Great Leap Forward was the most horrendous, claiming an estimated 20 million lives. While the Mao regime certainly exploited the people it ruled, and especially the rural people who put it in power in the first place, the Communist state was not the sole beneficiary of industrialization. During the Mao era significant improvements were made in diet, welfare, health care, and education (especially at the primary level), resulting in a dramatic near-doubling of average life expectancy—from 35 years in pre-1949 China to 65 years in 1976. Moreover, the collectivistic social achievements under Mao greatly facilitated the spectacular economic gains of the market reform era that followed. As Amartya Sen, the Noble Prize–winning Cambridge economist, has forcefully argued, the extensive development of public education, health care, and social security during the Mao era (in contrast to India's meager accomplishments in these areas) was crucial in promoting and sustaining economic growth in the Deng era.

MODERNIZATION UNDER MAO

Mao Zedong, whatever other judgments historians might render about his reign, will surely be counted among the great modernizers in history. He led a revolution that created the essential conditions for modern industrial development in a land that is the world's most populous—and one of its poorest. He also presided over 25 years of exceptionally rapid economic growth. Needless to say, many economic failures occurred as well, especially the sluggish growth of agriculture and the inability to make a decisive break with the Soviet-borrowed model of industrial organization. But with the very large exception of the human disaster that resulted from the Great Leap, the Maoist economic record is, on the whole, highly successful, especially when placed against the wretchedly low starting point from which China began its industrialization drive and the hostile international environment that so burdened the People's Republic in its early decades.

The great failure of Maoism was not economic but political. Not only did the Maoist regime fail to realize the democratic hopes aroused by the revolution, it also failed to fulfill its socialist promises. Mao's China was not socialist. It lacked, in both conception and reality, the essential feature of a socialist society, traditionally conceived as a system whereby the immediate producers control the conditions and products of their labor. Nor was there any conception, much less the reality, of the democratic political form that such a socialist society necessarily would assume, what Marx termed "the self-government of the producers."

Thus it was not the case, as charged by some and celebrated by others, that Deng Xiaoping's market reforms dismantled the socialism of the Mao era. In truth, there was no socialist system to destroy. Historical accuracy is ill-served by the conventional image of Mao as an ideological fanatic who sacrificed modern economic development to an all-consuming quest for a socialist spiritual utopia. Precisely the opposite would be closer to the historical record. It was more often the case that socialist goals and values were sacrificed to the imperatives of economic development.

While the Maoist economic record was impressive in its time, that time had passed by the early 1970s. Maoism had exhausted its once great creative energies and was no longer capable of providing inspiration to an increasingly disillusioned population. The modern industrial plant, now large, was also cumbersome and increasingly inefficient, requiring ever-larger infusions of capital to maintain high rates of growth. The Maoist method of financing industrialization—essentially state exploitation of the villages—could not have continued long without pauperizing the peasantry, the social base of the Communist revolution and the Maoist regime. But a dogmatized Maoism was no longer capable of new initiatives. It fell to Deng Xiaoping to bring about the necessary fundamental changes for the survival of the regime and the preservation of the material gains of the revolution.

Mao's Victims

Jonathan Mirsky

Harvard scholar Jonathan Mirsky argues that the fiftieth anniversary of the Communist takeover in China marks fifty years of terror and suffering more than of progress and achievement. He castigates Mao Zedong as nothing more than a tyrant who had no political thought system other than to stay in power and rid himself of rivals. Mirsky recounts the many purges initiated by Mao to rid himself of enemies; purges that began long before Mao took power. Millions died from famine because of Mao's misbegotten economic theories, and millions more died during the Cultural Revolution, which Mao fostered in his attempts to maintain control of China. Indeed, Mirsky claims, the Communist Party's attempt to legitimize "Mao Zedong Thought" is really an attempt to hang on to power.

"A revolution is not a dinner party. . . . [I]t is an act of violence by which one class overthrows another." During the 1960s, when the quotations of Chairman Mao enjoyed a certain vogue and many "progressives" in the West owned personal copies of Mao's "Little Red Book," this 1927 aphorism was a favorite. Few considered the word "violence"; if they did, they might have felt a frisson of vicarious excitement.

Today [October 1999] with the Communist authorities in China about to stage a huge celebration in honor of the fiftieth anniversary of the founding of the People's Republic of China [1949]—a revolution whose origins lie in the founding of the Chinese Communist Party almost 80 years ago—we have no excuse for failing to grasp the full significance of Mao Zedong's words. Having read a melange of Marxist texts, the young Mao could toss around words such as rich, middle, and poor peasants; national bourgeoisie; and big and middle landlords; and, in a godlike way, he could pro-

Jonathan Mirsky, "Nothing to Celebrate," *The New Republic*, vol. 221, October 11, 1999, p. 30. Copyright © 1999 by *The New Republic*. Reproduced by permission.

nounce that some would survive and others would be "overthrown." But what Mao actually meant by "class" was a sort, a kind, a category, with no Leninist attributions. He meant his enemies. And, since this category could, as it happened, include almost anyone, the "act of violence" Mao proposed would prove to be a more or less endless series of violent acts—going back to well before that fabled day, October 1, 1949, when he came to Tiananmen Square and declared that "the Chinese people have stood up."

WESTERN ACADEMIC ASSESSMENT OF MAO

From the purges that began even before Mao arrived at his mountain redoubt at Yenan, to the tragedy of the Cultural Revolution, the process of political transformation Mao and his comrades set in motion is a long story of intentional crimes and disastrous ideologically driven policy mistakes. Liquidation, survival, sometimes rehabilitation, more liquidation: This is the historical rhythm of the revolution Mao's heirs invite us to commemorate today.

Should we join in the celebration nonetheless? Many in the West seem prepared to answer at least a qualified yes. From academia comes the verdict of historian Maurice Meisner of the University of Wisconsin, who, in a recent lecture in London, justified the Chinese Revolution on the grounds of historical necessity. Meisner maintains that the Chinese Revolution did more for "people than any other single political event in world history." He concedes that the revolution was accompanied by "horrors and crimes," including the gulag, purges, famine and "the denial of basic rights of free expression and association." But, given the corruption of [Nationalist leader] Chiang Kai-shek, the brutality of Japanese occupation and the effectiveness of Mao's army in combating it, and the seemingly incurable chaos and stagnation that had enveloped China after the fall of the Manchu dynasty in 1911, there "was no real alternative" to this "most heroic of revolutions." What has happened in China, Meisner contends, already is plainly "the most massive and most popular revolution in world history."

To be sure, Meisner is an old enthusiast of left-wing revolutions, although many respectable sinologists of every ideological stripe have shared his basic verdict for years. Yet the celebratory mood runs strong even—or perhaps especially—among the top ranks of American capitalism. Here the excitement stems not so much from an evaluation of China's history but rather from an assessment of its future—as a huge market. China's modernization under communism, especially the last 20 years of rapid growth under a more market-oriented party leadership, also impresses the world's giant corporations. . . .

It was Mao's faithful acolyte Zhou Enlai who once said that it was still too early to tell the historical significance of the French Revolution. In this sense, China's rulers and their friends around the world seem to be rushing to judgment. For there is another view of what this fiftieth anniversary is really about, a view of China's revolution that regards the awful human suffering that accompanied it as neither historically determined nor justified by the undeniable economic improvements of the past two decades, advances that have been accompanied by some loosening of the once-total grip the Communist Party maintained over every facet of daily life in China.

No one can say where China would be today if the Communists had not taken over. Perhaps its economic stagnation and political chaos would have deepened. Perhaps it would have slowly developed into a modern, democratic capitalist state like South Korea or Taiwan. Or perhaps the best verdict is that China's revolution was a human catastrophe of unequalled scope—a colossal political, economic, and moral setback from which the society is still recovering. It is, moreover, a recovery to which the Chinese Communist Party, for all the positive developments of the past 20 years, is still an obstacle.

FUTIAN INCIDENT

Any view that Mao's depredations were necessitated by the war with Chiang, the Japanese occupation, China's sheer backwardness and disorder, or, perhaps, the later hostility of Russia and the United States cannot be squared with a simple fact: the party's ugliest and most systematic violence was always reserved for those within its own ranks, and this internecine cruelty began too early to allow it to be chalked up to outside pressures or political necessity. What Harvard University's Roderick MacFarquhar calls "the mark of Cain" stained the party as early as 1930, 19 years before Mao came to power, when Mao's infant Red Army crushed a rival provincial Communist force known as the AB Corps. The party accused the corps of being counterrevolutionary and executed hundreds of its members.

At the center of this struggle was an "incident" in a town called Futian. The leading scholar of the purge, Stephen Averill, says, "There is no reason whatsoever to think there was ever an elaborate multi-tiered secret AB Corps network plotting the destruction of the revolution," as Mao had alleged. Averill quotes Xiao Ke, one of the party's earliest military leaders: "We comrades who participated in this movement, regardless of whether we were executors or victims, all remember . . . that aside from oral confessions there was really no evidence to prove the existence of [the AB Corps]. Today, fifty years later . . . we still cannot find any concrete evidence proving the existence of [the AB Corps] in the Soviet areas at that time."

VIOLENCE AND FAMINE

Futian foreshadowed the killings at Yenan, the mountain province to which Mao dragged the tired and purged remnants of his party after the Long March of 1934–1935. For the eleven years from 1936 until 1947, the headquarters at Yenan became a scene of periodic and bloody internal killing. For their invaluable book, *Revolutionary Discourse in Mao's Republic*, David Apter of Yale and Tony Saich, now at Harvard, interviewed 150 veterans of Yenan: peasants, workers, soldiers, teachers, writers, underground workers, one of Mao's secretaries, and Mao's photographers, together with "some very angry widows, survivors of those whose faction, or unit, had been on the losing side in the internal struggles for power within the [party]." Apter and Saich note: "Very few of those interviewed had been exempt from physical abuse and verbal assault . . . all had survived by learning how to keep their mouths shut, except to parrot the appropriate line and use the exact words, phrases, and expressions countenanced by the authorities."

Apter and Saich point out that Mao engaged in four key contests for power at Yenan. "Each of the four struggles ended in the death or exile of Mao's designated opponent. In each case his victory was complete. . . . By demolishing anyone who dared to challenge him . . . Mao was able to position himself not only as a locus of power within the party, but also as a source of power in and of himself. . . ." The leading specialist in China on the Yenan purges is the scientist and journalist Dai Qing, who has written of the beheading, drowning, and burying alive of "Trotskyists." This was the place where [American journalist] Edgar Snow discovered an inspirational "red star over China" and where Foreign Service Officer John S. Service, who was stationed there for some months, found "a ymca camp." Service told me years later that he had subsequently learned of the killing, but that even if he had known about it at the time he would have ignored it, since, in his mind, everything had to be subordinated to beating the Japanese.

Once in power, the Chinese Communist Party continued its destructive work. Beginning in the late 1950s, having already driven the Dalai Lama into his Indian exile, Beijing set about dismantling Buddhism's works and clergy, which are the core and the rationale of Tibetan life. The Communist Chinese takeover of Tibet was an act of crude nationalistic conquest admitting of no defensible explanation in terms of Beijing's political or economic self-interest. It changed the traditionally self-sufficient economy of the region so that for at least 15 years there was mass famine. This policy has been compounded by the transplanting of tens of thousands of Chinese into Tibet, where the native people are in danger of becoming a minority. The notion that, by clinging to their unique civilization, the Tibetans are "interfering with politics and education" is the justification for the enormities that have kept the jails of Tibet well-stocked with Buddhist nuns and priests.

We know from the seminal study *Chinese Village, Socialist State* by Edward Friedman, Mark Selden, and Paul Pickowicz, that, even before it took power in Beijing, the party encouraged local thugs to kill its targets and in "model villages" advanced policies that it knew were catastrophic but could not admit had failed. Hundreds of thousands of landlords—rich and not so rich—were killed in the early '50s after the Maoist victory. Perhaps a half-million people were purged during the two-year anti-rightist drive that began in 1957. Many died—either through murder or inhuman treatment—in labor camps. All of this set the stage for the largest famine in human history, known as the Three Terrible Years, which lasted from 1959 to 1961.

In the third volume of his masterful *The Origins of the Cultural Revolution*, MacFarquhar writes that, in 1959 and 1960, in a single county—Fengyang in Anhui province—60,245 people, 17.7 percent of the population, died. In some communes, between 20 and 30 percent of the population perished. Conditions were so grim in one place, according to MacFarquhar, "that a scholar of ancient Chinese history compared this village to a neolithic site. . . ." In a normal year, 250,000 people died in Anhui. In 1960, 2,200,000 died of hunger there. In Sichuan province, China's most populous, the population sank from 70,810,000 to 64,591,800 between 1957 and 1961. During the same period, at least 13 provinces recorded negative population growth. In Beijing, the annual number of deaths rose from 320,000 in 1957 to 790,000 in 1961, the year in which Snow, who was visiting China, poured scorn on those who claimed Chinese were starving. MacFarquhar quotes estimates that 30 million died. China's leading investigative journalist, Liu Binyan, says that, in party circles at the time, the figure was believed to be 50 million.

THE CULTURAL REVOLUTION

During the Cultural Revolution, which ran from 1966 to 1976, millions are reported to have died, again either murdered or allowed to perish in confinement. The horrors of the Cultural Revolution were legion. Twenty years ago in Beijing, I watched the televised Gang of Four trial, at which witness after witness described torture and execution. Many of the interrogations had been recorded on tape so that Madame Mao could listen to them at her convenience. She defended her actions to the judges, saying, "I was just Chairman Mao's lapdog. Whom he said I should bite, I bit." Zhou Enlai, supposed by some to have protected potential victims during these years, in fact chaired a committee that oversaw the harsh treatment of Mao's specially selected victims, meticulously carrying out his wishes. Two years ago, I heard a Chinese scholar now at the University of California at Berkeley describe the dozens of schools that had been seized by Red Guards and Maoist "work teams," where the killing of teachers was frequent and where no one who witnessed the violence could recall a single dissenting voice raised in the victims' defense.

COMMUNIST PARTY ASSESSMENT OF MAO

And what of China's official efforts truthfully to assess these horrendous deeds and the question of who bears the responsibility for them? In June 1981, five years after Mao's death, the party, now in the hands of Deng Xiaoping and his colleagues, published an account of its own history since its founding. This extraordinary 32-page document was edited carefully by Deng himself. It starts off on a dishonest note, praising the pre-1949 years of the insurrectionist party. Indeed, the Deng-edited document obfuscates the very origins of the party, claiming almost 60 members founded it in 1921. The party was actually founded in 1920 by two or three revolutionaries who were cast out in the early years; it became necessary for party historians to record that the founding took place in 1921, when Mao was present. The report describes Mao's first great purge of intellectuals, at Yenan in 1942, as "a tremendous success," although it set the stage for intellectual purges to this day.

The candor begins, barely, with an account of 1956 in which the document concedes that after "the socialist transformation of the private ownership of the means of production . . . there had been shortcomings and errors. . . . [W]e were far from meticulous, the changes were too fast. . . ." This refers to the establishment of the agricultural cooperatives, forerunners to the disastrous communes of 1958, which were a key factor in the subsequent famines and a "shortcoming" not reversed until the late '70s. Regarding the anti-rightist campaign, launched in 1957 after Mao determined that the Hundred Flowers period—when intellectuals were encouraged to criticize the leadership—had gone too far, Deng's history has this to say: "A handful of bourgeois Rightists seized the opportunity to advocate what they called 'speaking out and airing views in a big way,' and to mount a wild attack against the Party. . . . It was therefore entirely correct and necessary to launch a resolute counterattack. But the scope of this struggle was far too broad and a number of intellectuals, patriotic people, and Party cadres were unjustifiably labeled 'Rightists,' with unfortunate consequences." This dainty phrase refers to the vast purging of an estimated 500,000 people, including the current premier, Zhu Rongji—many of whom were detained until well after the Cultural Revolution ended in 1976.

The document then turns to the years 1958–1960, known as the Great Leap Forward ("mistakes of enlarging the scope of class struggle and of impetuosity and rashness in economic construction"), a period marked by "arbitrary directions, boastfulness, and the stirring up of a 'communist wind'.

. . . Comrade Mao Zedong and many leading comrades both at the center and in the localities . . . overestimated the role of man's subjective will and efforts." The document admits that the charges drawn up against old revolutionary comrades who dared to criticize Mao "were entirely wrong." Yet there is no mention of the tens of millions who perished of hunger during those years. To this day, that disaster is barely mentioned. When it is, it is understated, and the Soviet Union is blamed for cutting off economic aid.

Creeping towards "the comprehensive, long-drawn-out, and grave blunder"—the Cultural Revolution—the document admits that, during the early '60s, "'Left' errors . . . actually grew in the spheres of politics, ideology, and politics." Between 1964 and 1965, "a number of the cadres at grassroots levels were unjustly dealt with. . . ." (There are no details about how they were "dealt with.") The account of the Cultural Revolution fills seven pages, summed up with the following: "The 'cultural revolution' which lasted from May 1966 to October 1976 was responsible for the most severe setback and the heaviest losses suffered by the Party, the state, and the people since the founding of the People's Republic. It was initiated and led by Comrade Mao Zedong." The document adds, "Comrade Mao Zedong must be held chiefly responsible. . . . [H]is personal arbitrariness gradually undermined democratic centralism in Party life and the personality cult grew graver and graver."

Yet, even here, there is a crucial weasel phrase. Having derided the major ideas of the decade [1966–1976], the document says that "these theses must be thoroughly distinguished from Mao Zedong Thought." Mao—but not his "Thought"—was responsible, the document admits, for errors long before 1966. But they were the errors "of a great proletarian revolutionary. . . . Herein lies his tragedy. . . . His merits are primary and his errors secondary." As for the party itself: "Without the Chinese Communist Party there would have been no new China. . . . [I]t can correct its mistakes and in no case should one use the Party's mistakes as a pretext for weakening, breaking away from or even sabotaging its leadership."

Even if some of Communist China's foreign apologists can posit a radical discontinuity between the awful past and the promising present, China's own leaders know better. They know that a completely candid assessment of their performance would have to go right back to the origins of the party and would implicate Mao personally in campaign after campaign of mass murder and devastating policy errors. And, if Mao is to blame, then the party he built is to blame; and if the party is to blame, then those who inherited its revolutionary mantle have no legitimate claim to rule. . . .

In short, Mao's trivial "Thought" and his actual record of governance, ghastly as it is, are all China's current rulers have in the way of a claim to legitimacy. Little wonder, that Vice President Hu Jintao, a member of the party's powerful Politburo [who became head of the CCP in November 2002], recently told students at the party school: "Party leaders at all levels should improve their study of Marxism, Leninism, Mao Zedong Thought, and particularly Deng Xiaoping theory, so as to sharpen their political consciousness."

The Memory of Mao

Philip Short

Philip Short, in his monumental biography of Chairman Mao, reviews the many ways Mao will be remembered: by his prodigious talents, by his accomplishments, and most of all, by his many victims. Mao himself saw the parallel between his rule and the brutal rule of China's first emperor, Qin Shihuangdi (259–209 B.C.). The Qin emperor unified China, as did Mao, and his short reign preceded one of China's greatest Golden Ages, the Han (202 B.C.–A.D. 220). Short, a foreign correspondent who has reported for the London *Times* and the British Broadcasting Company, asks the intriguing question: Will Mao's rule be followed by another golden age in Chinese history or will Mao be remembered as a "failed colossus"?

The achievements of Mao's great contemporaries, Roosevelt, Churchill and De Gaulle, are measured against those of their peers. Even Stalin built on Lenin's accomplishments. Mao's life was played out on an altogether vaster canvas. He was unquestioned leader of almost a quarter of mankind, inhabiting an area the size of Europe. He wielded powers equalled only by the most awesome of Chinese emperors, in an era when China's history was so compressed that changes which, in the West, had taken centuries to accomplish, occurred in a single generation. In Man's lifetime, China made the leap from semi-colony to Great Power; from millennial autarky [economic self-sufficiency] to socialist state; from despoiled victim of imperialist plunder to Permanent Member of the UN Security Council, complete with H-bombs, surveillance satellites and ICBMS.

Mao had an extraordinary mix of talents: he was visionary, statesman, political and military strategist of genius, philosopher and poet. Foreigners might sniff. In a memorable putdown, Arthur Waley, the great translator of Tang dynasty poetry, described Mao's poems as 'not as bad as Hitler's paintings, but not as good as Churchill's'. In the judgement of another Western art historian, his calligraphy, while 'strikingly original, betraying a flamboyant egotism, to the point of arrogance, if not extravagance . . . [and] a total disregard for the formal discipline of the brush', was 'essentially inarticulate'. Most Chinese scholars disagree, Mao's poems, like his brushwork, seized the tormented, restless spirit of his age.

To these gifts, he brought a subtle, dogged mind, awe-inspiring charisma and fiendish cleverness.

THE FIRST EMPEROR AND MAO

The philippic [denunciation] penned by Lin Biao's son [Lin Liguo]—'Today he uses sweet words and honeyed talk to those whom he entices; tomorrow he puts them to death for fabricated crimes'—unconsciously echoed the judgement two thousand years earlier of an adviser to Qin Shihuangdi, the greatest of China's founding emperors. 'The King of Qin is [like] a bird of prey . . . There is no beneficence in him, and he has the heart of a tiger or a wolf. When he is in difficulties, he finds it easy to humble himself. But when he has achieved his aim, he finds it just as easy to devour human beings . . . If [he] realises his ambitions concerning the Empire, all men will be his slaves'.

Mao knew by heart the lessons of the dynastic histories. It was not chance that led him to choose, among all his imperial predecessors, the First Emperor of Qin—who throughout Chinese history had been feared and reviled as the epitome of harsh rule—as the man against whom he wished to measure himself. 'You accuse us of acting like Qin Shihuangdi', he once told a group of liberal intellectuals. 'You are wrong. We surpass him a hundred times. When you berate us for imitating his despotism, we are happy to agree! Your mistake was that you did not say so enough'.

To Mao, the killing of opponents—or simply of those who disagreed with his political aims—was an unavoidable, indeed a necessary, ingredient of broader political campaigns.

He rarely gave direct instruction for their physical elimination.[1] But his rule brought about the deaths of more of his own people than any other leader in history.

---

1. Mao's direct involvement in the hunting down and execution of presumed opponents was limited to the period from 1930–31 in the Jiangxi base area. In the Yan'an Rectification Campaign, he gave instructions that 'no cadre is to be killed', but, in practice, allowed [Politburo member and Mao's hatchetman] Kang Sheng to drive Party dissidents to suicide. This pattern was repeated throughout his leadership of the People's Republic.

Mao's Victims

The victims of the land reform, of his political campaigns—the 'movement to suppress counter-revolutionaries'; the 'Three Antis'; the 'Five Antis'; the anti-Rightist Campaign; the movement against 'Right opportunism'; the Socialist Education Movement; the Cultural Revolution; the campaign against 'May 16' elements; and the 'cleansing of class ranks', to mention but the most important—and of the famines triggered by the Great Leap Forward, have been exceeded only once—by all the dead of the Second World War.

By comparison, Stalin's liquidation of the kulaks [land owners] and his destruction of the Russian intelligentsia in the labour camps, claimed 12 to 15 million victims; Hitler's holocaust, less than half that number.

Those parallels, while persuasive, are in one important sense false, however. Stalin set out deliberately to encompass the physical extermination of all who stood in his way. . . . Hitler's 'final solution' was designed to extirpate in the gas chambers an entire racial group—the Jews—whose genetic stock besmirched his new Aryan world order.

The overwhelming majority of those whom Mao's policies killed were unintended casualties of famine. The others—three or four million of them—were the human detritus, of his epic struggle to transform China.

That was cold comfort for his victims; nor did it diminish in any way the egregious misery that Mao's colossal effort of social engineering caused. But it put him in a different category from other twentieth-century tyrants. Just as, in law, there is a capital distinction between murder, manslaughter, and death caused by negligence, so in politics there are gradations of responsibility, related to motivation and intent, for leaders who bring massive suffering to their peoples.

Stalin cared about what his subjects did (or might do); Hitler, about who they were. Mao cared about what they thought.

China's landlords were eliminated as a class (and many of them were killed in the process); but they were not exterminated as a people, as the Jews were in Germany. Even as his policies caused the deaths of millions, Mao never entirely lost his belief in the efficacy of thought reform and the possibility of redemption. 'Heads are not like chives', he said. 'They do not grow back again'.

MAO'S ACHIEVEMENTS

What was achieved at the cost of such bloodshed and pain?

Mao's own judgement, that his two major accomplishments were his victory over Chiang Kai-shek and the launching of the Cultural Revolution, offers a partial answer, though not quite in the sense he had intended. The one reunified China after a century of division and restored its sovereignty; the other gave the Chinese people such an overdose of ideological fervour as to immunise them for generations to come. Mao's tragedy and his grandeur were that he remained to the end in thrall to his own revolutionary dreams. Where Confucius had taught harmony—the doctrine of the mean—Mao preached endless class struggle, until it became a cage from which neither he nor the Chinese people could escape. He freed China from the straitjacket of its Confucian past. But the bright Red future he promised turned out to be a sterile purgatory.

So culminated a process of national disillusionment that had begun at the time of Mao's birth, when nineteenth-century reformers, responding to the clash with the West, for the first time challenged the beliefs that had kept the Chinese system frozen in immobility for the previous two thousand years.

After Mao, there was no new emperor—merely a succession of fallible leaders, not better and not worse than in any other country. Blind faith and ideology died. People began thinking for themselves. The old world had been smashed; the new had been found wanting. After a century of turmoil, China was ready to make a fresh start.

CHINA'S GOLDEN AGES

Revolution has more to do with tearing down the old than with painstakingly constructing the new. Mao's legacy was to clear the way for less visionary, more practical men to build the shining future that he could never achieve.

Twice before in Chinese history, radical despotisms have ushered in long periods of peace and prosperity. The First Emperor of Qin unified the feudal princedoms in the third century BC but his dynasty survived for only fifteen years. He paved the way for the Han, the first Golden Age of Chinese antiquity, which endured four centuries. In the sixth and early seventh centuries AD, the Sui, who reunified China after a time of division and instability known as the Six Dynasties and the Three Kingdoms, ruled for thirty-nine years. They were followed by the Tang, the second Golden Age, which lasted for three centuries. Mao ruled for twenty-seven years. If the past, as he believed, is indeed a mirror for the present, will the twenty-first century mark the start of a third Chinese golden age, for which the Maoist dictatorship will have opened the way?

Or will it be his fate to be remembered as a flawed colossus, who brought fundamental change on a scale that only a handful of others had managed in all the years of China's history, but then failed to follow through?

HOW MAO IS REMEMBERED

In December 1993, during celebrations marking the centenary of Mao's birth, a private soirée was held at Maxim's, in the business district of the new capitalist Beijing. It is a carbon copy of the restaurant on the Rue Royale in Paris, with the same heavy *belle époque* panelling, rococo silverware and velvet hangings, and similar prices. The two hundred invited guests were a cross-section of the city's moneyed aristocracy: private entrepreneurs in dark suits with foreign labels sewn ostentatiously on to the cuffs, and chunky gold watches on their wrists; stars of China's new film industry; actresses with curled hair; willowy fashion models. Among them was a Mao look-alike named Gu Yue, who had played the eponymous hero in a hagiographic television series depicting the communists' struggle for power. The official entertainment that night, to create the right mood of nostalgia and irony, was one of Jiang Qing's dreary revolutionary operas. After it was over, Gu and half-a-dozen friends, mellowed by champagne and cognac, climbed on to the stage and began to chant together the old Red Guard refrain. 'Mao Zedong Thought lights the way ahead'. As they did so, they blundered about like blind men bumping into each other in the dark. The audience collapsed. The leader they had once revered was now a laughing-stock.

For others, Mao became an icon. Taxi-drivers hung his portrait from their windscreens, suspended like an image of the Buddha on a chain of rosary beads. China's teenyboppers, too young to be burdened with memories of what life under the Chairman was really like, swapped Mao badges and memorabilia. Pop singers parodied his poems; painters reworked his image; designers put him everywhere, from dresses to eiderdowns.

In the countryside, Mao's smooth, unfathomable face continues to hold pride of place in innumerable homes. In Hunan, a temple with a 20-foot-high statue of him, flanked by seated effigies of Zhou Enlai and Zhu De, commissioned by local peasant associations from a sculptor at the Buddhist monastery on Wutaishan, attracted tens of thousands of visitors every day—until the Party ordered it closed for encouraging 'feudal superstition'.

The wheel had gone full circle. Mao had entered the pantheon of gods and folk-heroes, outlaws and brigands, who had peopled the dreams of his childhood at the start of his own long life of rebellion, a hundred years before.

History is laid down slowly in China. A final verdict on Mao's place in the annals of his country's past is still a very long way off.

BIOGRAPHIES OF MAJOR FIGURES IN THE MAOIST ERA

Cai Yuanpei (1868–1940): One of the May Fourth Movement intellectuals, he was educated in Europe. He then fostered an intellectual climate at Beijing (Peking) University during his tenure as chancellor.

Chen Boda (1904–1989): Mao's political secretary at Yanan base. He was the head of the Cultural Revolution Group in 1966 but was purged in 1970. Chen was subsequently imprisoned for political crimes but was released due to ill health.

Chen Duxiu (1879–1942): A radical Chinese intellectual educated in Europe, he criticized the feudalism of Confucianism in his magazine *New Youth* and influenced the May Fourth Movement participants. He and Li Dazhao were co-founders of the Chinese Communist Party.

Chen Yun (1905–1995): Chen was a Communist hard-liner who participated in the Long March and held various positions in the government related to economics. He was a rival of Deng Xiaoping.

Chiang Kai-shek (1887–1975): A military and political leader of the Nationalist (Guomindang) Party, Chiang struggled against and lost control of China to Mao Zedong and the Communists. He fled to Taiwan and ruled there as a dictator until his death.

Deng Xiaoping (1904–1997): Deng came from a wealthy peasant family in Sichuan province and studied in France in the 1920s. He joined the Jiangxi Soviet and went on the Long March. By 1956 he was general secretary of the Chinese Communist Party and implemented the Anti-Rightist Movement initiated by Mao. He advocated freer market policies during the Great Leap Forward famine. Because of this, he was purged during the Cultural Revolution, reinstated, and purged again. He came into power and took control of China in 1977 after Mao's death. He initiated many reforms in the Chinese economy and opened China to the outside world. He also ordered the notorious Tiananmen Square massacre of student protesters on June 4, 1989.

Hua Guofeng (1921–): Once designated heir to Mao Zedong, he lost the power struggle to Deng Xiaoping after Mao's death.

Hu Jintao (1942–): Hu served in various positions, including party secretary, in Tibet during the 1987–1989 uprising (which ended in the declaration of martial law and suppression of the protests). He was designated heir to Jiang Zemin and was elevated to the position of Communist Party chief in 2002.

Hu Shi (1891–1962): A Chinese intellectual educated in the United States, Hu was a participant in the May Fourth Movement, advocated the plain-language movement, and opposed communism.

Hu Yaobang (1915–1989): A moderate and an ally of Deng Xiaoping, Hu replaced Huang Guofeng as Chinese Communist Party chairman in 1981. He was later dismissed by Deng in 1987. He died in April 1989. Students mourning his death led to the Tiananmen Square protest and subsequent massacre on June 4, 1989.

Jiang Qing (1914–1991): Jiang was a Shanghai actress who married Mao in 1938 at Yanan. She became politically powerful during the Cultural Revolution as head of the extreme leftist Gang of Four. She committed suicide in prison.

Jiang Zemin (1926–): The third major leader of the People's Republic of China after Mao Zedong and Deng Xiaoping, Jiang continued Deng's economic policies.

Kang Sheng (1898–1975): Kang was the security chief of the CCP in Shanghai, a Politiburo member, and acted as hatchet man for Mao at Yanan and during the Cultural Revolution.

Li Dazhao (1888–1927): Li was the librarian at Beijing University, the leader in the May Fourth Movement, the supervisor of young library assistant Mao Zedong, and, along with Chen Duxiu, a cofounder of the Chinese Communist Party. He was executed by warlord Zhang Zuolin in 1927.

Lin Biao (1907–1971): A Chinese military commander and Politburo member, Lin helped to bring about Communist military victories over the Nationalists. He assisted in the construction of the Mao cult. Designated Mao's successor, Lin later rebelled against Mao. He died while attempting to flee China for the Soviet Union in 1971.

Li Peng (1928–): Li became premier of China in 1987 and served in that position for ten years. He was humiliated in a 1989 televised debate with Tiananmen Square student protesters. He is often referred to as "the Butcher of Beijing" for his role in unleashing the military on student protesters on June 4, 1989.

Liu Bochen (1892–1986): Liu was a Red Army military leader and Politburo member.

Liu Shaoqi (1898–1969): Liu was a Communist leader who served with Mao at Yanan, was designated Mao's heir, and became head of the PRC in 1959. He was purged in the Cultural Revolution for taking he "capitalist road." He died of medical neglect.

Lu Xun (1881–1936): Lu was a leftist writer who influenced the May Fourth Movement.

Peng Dehuai (1898–1974): Peng was a military commander who fought in the Sino-Japanese war and in the Korean War. He was a Politburo member who criticized Mao for his Great Leap Forward policies. He was purged in 1966 during the Cultural Revolution and later died in a prison hospital from medical neglect.

Qin Shihuangdi (259–209 B.C.): China's first emperor, Qin was a brutal ruler who suppressed all opposition, unified China, and established legalism as the ruling philosophy.

Sun Yat-sen (1866–1925): Sun was a medical doctor and political thinker who led a campaign to overthrow the Qing dynasty and establish the Republic of China. He is known as the father of modern China and founded the Guomindang (Nationalist Party).

Wang Hongwen (1933–1992): A Communist cadre leader and potential successor to Mao in 1972, arrested as one of the Gang of Four after Mao's death. He died in prison.

Yao Wenyuan (1925–): Yao was a radical literary critic and Politburo member. He helped Mao launch the Cultural Revolution and was arrested after Mao's death as one of the Gang of Four. He was imprisoned, later released on parole, and now lives in Shanghai.

Zhang Chunqiao (1917–): A Communist propaganda officer, Zhang became a leader in the Cultural Revolution, and later a Politburo member. He was arrested as a member of the Gang of Four after Mao's death and received a commuted death sentence for political crimes.

Zhou Enlai (1898–1976): Zhou was a Politburo member and the prime minister of China from 1949 until his death of cancer in 1976. He served as Mao's primary aid and adviser most of his life but always took a subordinate role. He was intensely loyal to Mao Zedong and second in command of China during Mao's regime.

Zhu Rongji (1929–): Zhu joined the party in 1949 and worked for the State Planning Commission. He was purged during the Anti-Rightist Movement and was later allowed to rejoin the State Planning Commission. He became mayor of Shanghai in 1987 and China's prime minister in 1997.

APPENDIX OF DOCUMENTS

DOCUMENT 1: REMEMBERING A PEASANT REBELLION

As a youth, Mao was deeply impressed by the suppression of a peasant rebellion in his home province. He told this story to journalist Edgar Snow, who interviewed Mao in Shaanxi in the 1930s.

"At this time [ca. 1908] an incident occurred in Hunan which influenced my whole life. Outside the little Chinese school where I was studying, we students noticed many bean merchants coming back from Changsha. We asked them why they were all leaving. They told us about a big uprising in the city.

"There had been a severe famine that year, and in Changsha thousands were without food. The starving sent a delegation to the civil governor to beg for relief, but he replied to them haughtily, 'Why haven't you food? There is plenty in the city. I always have enough.' When the people were told the governor's reply, they became very angry. They held mass meetings and organized a demonstration. They attacked the Manchu yamen [Qing dynasty officials], cut down the flagpole, the symbol of office, and drove out the governor. Following this, the Commissioner of Internal Affairs, a man named Chang, came out on his horse and told the people that the government would take measures to help them. Chang was evidently sincere in his promise, but the Emperor disliked him and accused him of having intimate connections with 'the mob.' He was removed. A new governor arrived, and at once ordered the arrest of the leaders of the uprising. Many of them were beheaded and their heads displayed on poles as a warning to future 'rebels.'

"This incident was discussed in my school for many days. It made a deep impression on me. Most of the other students sympathized with the 'insurrectionists,' but only from an observer's point of view. They did not understand that it had any relation to their own lives. They were merely interested in it as an exciting incident. I never forgot it. I felt that there with the rebels were ordinary people like my own family and I deeply resented the injustice of the treatment given to them.

Edgar Snow, *Red Star over China.* New York: Grove Press, 1968.

DOCUMENT 2: INTELLECTUALS AND PEASANTS MUST UNITE

Mao believed the Communist revolution in China was the next stage in a process that began with the Revolution of 1911 and the May Fourth and New Culture Movements. In this excerpt from a newspaper article he wrote in 1939—on the twentieth anniversary of the May Fourth Movement—Mao calls on intellectuals to join the workers and peasants in ushering in the Communist state and overthrowing imperialist invaders.

The May 4th [1919] Movement twenty years ago marked a new stage in China's bourgeois-democratic revolution against imperialism and feudalism. The cultural reform movement which grew out of the May 4th Movement was only one of the manifestations of this revolution. With the growth and development of new social forces in that period, a powerful camp made its appearance in the bourgeois-democratic revolution, a camp consisting of the working class, the student masses and the new national bourgeoisie. Around the time of the May 4th Movement, hundreds of thousands of students courageously took their place in the van. In these respects the May 4th Movement went a step beyond the Revolution of 1911 [in which the Qing dynasty was overthrown]. . . .

China's democratic revolution depends on definite social forces for its accomplishment. These social forces are the working class, the peasantry, the intelligentsia and the progressive section of the bourgeoisie, that is, the revolutionary workers, peasants, soldiers, students and intellectuals, and businessmen, with the workers and peasants as the basic revolutionary forces and the workers as the class which leads the revolution. It is impossible to accomplish the anti-imperialist and anti-feudal democratic revolution without these basic revolutionary forces and without the leadership of the working class. Today, the principal enemies of the revolution are the Japanese imperialists and the Chinese traitors, and the fundamental policy in the revolution is the policy of the Anti-Japanese National United Front, consisting of all workers, peasants, soldiers, students and intellectuals, and businessmen who are against Japanese aggression. Final victory in the War of Resistance will be won when this united front is greatly consolidated and developed.

In the Chinese democratic revolutionary movement, it was the intellectuals who were the first to awaken. This was clearly demonstrated both in the Revolution of 1911 and in the May 4th Movement, and in the days of the May 4th Movement the intellectuals were more numerous and more politically conscious than in the days of the Revolution of 1911. But the intellectuals will accomplish nothing if they fail to integrate themselves with the workers and peasants. In the final analysis, the dividing line between revolutionary intellectuals and non-revolutionary or counter-revolutionary intellectuals is whether or not they are willing to integrate themselves with the workers and peasants and actually do so. Ultimately it is this alone, and not professions of faith in the Three People's Principles or in Marxism, that distinguishes one from the other. A true revolutionary must be one who is willing to integrate himself with the workers and peasants and actually does so.

Mao Zedong, "The May 4ᵗʰ Movement," in *Selected Works of Mao Tse-Tung*, vol. 2. Peking: Foreign Languages Press, 1967.

DOCUMENT 3: THE OPPRESSION OF WOMEN

Miss Zhao was a young woman who committed suicide rather than be forced into an arranged marriage with a man she did not love. Mao wrote several articles about this incident in which he debated the traditional subservient role of women in society. In this article, published November 21, 1919, Mao puts forth some of his views on women and gender relations.

In recent days there have been many commentaries on the incident of Miss Zhao's suicide, and I too have written a few comments on it that have been published in this city's *Dagongbao* [newspaper]. This is a public event that concerns all mankind, and leaving aside those who advocate extreme individualism and living alone, everyone should pay attention to it and study it. But Chinese women should devote particular attention and study to it. Because for several thousand years perverse customs based on the [Confucian] rites have prevailed in China, women have had no status in any area of life. From politics, law, and education, to business, social relations, entertainment, and personal status, women have always been treated very differently from men, and relegated to the dark corners of society. Not only are they denied happiness, they are also subjected to many kinds of inhumane mistreatment. That this incident of a woman being driven to suicide should occur at a time like this, when the truth is very clear and there are loud calls for the liberation of women, shows just how profound are the evils of our nation's society. Today we need not express more pity for the deceased, but rather we should look for a method that will thoroughly correct this problem so that from now on such a tragedy as this will never happen again. But before we look for a method, we must first search for the controlling root causes of this domination. . . .

The relationship between men and women should, according to the contemporary view, center on "love," and apart from love, must not be governed by "economics." Thus the contemporary position is, "Each is economically independent, sharing the fruits of love." Before modern times, this was not the case. No one knew of the principle "Love is sacred." In the relationship between men and women, love was considered to be only secondary, while the core relationship remained economic, and was thus controlled by capitalism. In antiquity, eating was a simple affair. People picked fruit and caught wild animals and fish, and were easily satisfied. Men and women were equals, and economically women asked nothing of men and men asked nothing of women. Men and women sought of each other only "love." Thus woman sometimes, on the contrary, used her physiological strengths (physiologists say that in sexual physiology women are stronger than men) to control men. Later, as population increased, and food supplies became inadequate, the competition for survival made it necessary to emphasize work, and with this arrived the terrible age in which women became subjugated to men.

In doing physical labor, women are not inherently inferior to men, but because women cannot work during the period of child-bearing, men took advantage of this weakness, exploited this single flaw, made "submission" the condition of exchange and used "food" to shut them up. This then is the general cause that has kept women subjugated and unable to emancipate themselves. On the one hand, what member of the human race was not born of woman? Childbearing by women is an indispensable element in the survival of humanity. That men should have forgotten this supreme act of benevolence, and on the contrary should have wantonly and unscrupulously oppressed them, merely for the sake of petty economic relationships, is truly a case of returning evil for good. On the other hand, childbearing is an extremely painful event. "The pangs of childbirth" is a term that frightens every woman who hears it. Despite the medical discoveries that have changed the "difficulty of childbirth" into the "ease of childbirth," we should show great reverence and compassion. How can we instead take advantage of trivial economic benefits to press the other down?

Having presented the "reasons" above, we can now turn to the "methods." The methods by which women can become free and independent and never again be oppressed by men may in general be listed as follows:

1) A woman must never marry before she is physically mature.

2) Before marriage, at the bare minimum, a woman must be adequately prepared in knowledge and skills to live her own life.

3) A woman must prepare herself for living expenses after childbirth.

The above three items are the basic prerequisites for a woman's own personal independence. In addition, there is a further condition of "public child support," to which society should pay close attention. If women themselves are able to fulfill the above three conditions, and if society, for its part, provides for the public rearing of children, then marital relationships centered on love can be established. This will depend on the efforts of all of us young men and women!

Mao Zedong, "Concerning the Incident of Miss Zhao's Suicide," in *Mao's Road to Power: Revolutionary Writings 1912–1949*, vol 1, ed. Stuart R. Schram. Armonk, NY: M.E. Sharpe, 1992.

DOCUMENT 4: A REVOLUTION IS NOT A DINNER PARTY

In one of Mao's most significant political works, he argues against those who criticize the peasant revolution in the late 1920s as unruly and going too far in obtaining retribution for past abuses at the hands of the landowners. Mao indicates his approval of using violence as a tactic to bring about social change when he says, "a revolution is not a dinner party. . . . A revolution is an insurrection, an act of violence by which one class overthrows another."

During my recent visit to Hunan [1927] I made a first-hand investigation of conditions in the five counties of Hsiangtan, Hsianghsiang, Hengshan, Liling and Changsha. In the thirty-two days from January 4 to February 5, I called together fact-finding conferences in villages and county towns, which were attended by experienced peasants and by comrades working in the peasant movement, and I listened attentively to their reports and collected a great deal of material. Many of the hows and whys of the peasant movement were the exact opposite of what the gentry in Hankow and Changsha are saying. I saw and heard of many strange things of which I had hitherto been unaware. I believe the same is true of many other places, too. All talk directed against the peasant movement must be speedily set right. All the wrong measures taken by the revolutionary authorities concerning the peasant movement must be speedily changed. Only thus can the future of the revolution be benefited. For the present upsurge of the peasant movement is a colossal event. In a very short time, in China's central, southern and northern provinces, several hundred million peasants will rise like a mighty storm, like a hurricane, a force so swift and violent that no power, however great, will be able to hold it back. They will smash all the trammels that bind them and rush forward along the road to liberation. They will sweep all the imperialists, warlords, corrupt officials, local tyrants and evil gentry into their graves. Every revolutionary party and every revolutionary comrade will be put to the test, to be accepted or rejected as they decide. There are three alternatives. To march at their head and lead them? To trail behind them, gesticulating and criticizing? Or to stand in their way and oppose them? Every Chinese is free to choose, but events will force you to make the choice quickly. . . .

THE QUESTION OF "GOING TOO FAR"

Then there is another section of people who say, "Yes, peasant associations are necessary, but they are going rather too far." This is the opinion of the middle-of-the-roaders. But what is the actual situation? True, the peasants are in a sense "unruly" in the countryside. . . . [The peasants in revolt] fine the local tyrants and evil gentry, they demand contributions from them, and they smash their sedan-chairs. People swarm into the houses of local tyrants and evil gentry who are against the peasant association, slaughter their pigs and consume their grain. They even loll for a minute or two on the ivory-inlaid beds belonging to the young ladies in the households of the local tyrants and evil gentry. At the slightest provocation they make arrests, crown the arrested with tall paperhats, and parade them through the villages, saying, "You dirty landlords, now you know who we are!" Doing whatever they like and turning everything upside down, they have created a kind of terror in the countryside. This is what some people call "going too far", or "exceeding the proper limits in righting a wrong", or "really too much". Such talk may seem plausible, but in fact it is wrong. First, the local tyrants, evil gentry and lawless landlords have themselves driven the peasants to this. For ages they have used their power to tyrannize over the peasants and trample them underfoot; that is why the peasants have reacted so strongly. The most violent revolts and the most serious disorders have invariably occurred in places where the local tyrants, evil gentry and lawless landlords perpetrated the worst outrages. The peasants are clear-sighted. Who is bad and who is not, who is the worst and who is not quite so vicious, who deserves severe punishment and who deserves to be let off lightly— the peasants keep clear accounts, and very seldom has the punishment exceeded the crime. Secondly, a revolution is not a dinner party, or writing an essay, or painting a picture, or doing embroidery; it cannot be so refined, so leisurely and gentle, so temperate, kind, courteous, restrained and magnanimous. A revolution is an insurrection, an act of violence by which one class overthrows another. A rural revolution is a revolution by which the peasantry overthrows the power of the feudal landlord class. Without using the greatest force, the peasants cannot possibly overthrow the deep-rooted authority of the landlords which has lasted for thousands of years. The rural areas need a mighty revolutionary upsurge, for it alone can rouse the people in their millions to become a powerful force. All the actions mentioned here which have been labelled as "going too far" flow from the power of the peasants, which has been called forth by the mighty revolutionary upsurge in the countryside. It was highly necessary for such things to be done in the second period of the peasant movement, the period of revolutionary action. In this period it was necessary to establish the absolute authority of the peasants. It was necessary to forbid malicious criticism of the peasant associations. It was necessary to overthrow the whole authority of the gentry, to strike them to the ground and keep them there. There is revolutionary significance in all the actions which were labelled as "going too far" in this period. To put it bluntly, it is necessary to create terror for a while in every rural area, or otherwise it would be impossible to suppress the activities of the counter-revolutionaries in the countryside or overthrow the authority of the gentry. Proper limits have to be exceeded in order to right a wrong, or else the wrong cannot be righted. Those who talk about the peasants "going too far" seem at first sight to be different from those who say "It's terrible!" as mentioned earlier, but in essence they proceed from the same standpoint and likewise voice a landlord theory that upholds the interests of the privileged classes. Since this theory impedes the rise of the peasant movement and so disrupts the revolution, we must firmly oppose it.

Mao Zedong, "Report on an Investigation of the Peasant Movement in Hunan," in *Selected Works of Mao Tse-Tung*, vol. 1. Peking: Foreign Languages Press, 1975.

DOCUMENT 5: ART SHOULD SERVE THE PEOPLE

While encamped in northern China, Mao conducted a rectification campaign to unify his followers' beliefs and bring them in line with Communist Party thinking. One of Mao's chief concerns was the "thought reform" of Chinese intellectuals. In the following speech given on May 2, 1942, Mao makes it clear that intellectual pursuits such as art and literature have only one purpose: to serve the working people.

Comrades! You have been invited to this forum today to exchange ideas and examine the relationship between work in the literary and artistic fields and revolutionary work in general. Our aim is to ensure that revolutionary literature and art follow the correct path of development and provide better help to other revolutionary work in facilitating the overthrow of our national enemy [the Japanese invaders] and the accomplishment of the task of national liberation.

In our struggle for the liberation of the Chinese people there are various fronts, among which there are the fronts of the pen and of the gun, the cultural and the military fronts. To defeat the enemy we must rely primarily on the army with guns. But this army alone is not enough; we must also have a cultural army, which is absolutely indispensable for uniting our own ranks and defeating the enemy. Since the May 4th Movement such a cultural army has taken shape in China, and it has helped the Chinese revolution, gradually reduced the domain of China's feudal culture and of the comprador culture which serves imperialist aggression, and weakened their influence. To oppose the new culture the Chinese reactionaries can now only "pit quantity against quality". In other words, reactionaries have money, and though they can produce nothing good, they can go all out and produce in quantity. Literature and art have been an important and successful part of the cultural front since the May 4th Movement. During the ten years' civil war, the revolutionary literature and art movement grew greatly. That movement and the revolutionary war both headed in the same general direction, but these two fraternal armies were not linked together in their practical work because the reactionaries had cut them off from each other. It is very good that since the outbreak of the War of Resistance Against Japan, more and more revolutionary writers and artists have been coming to Yenan and our other anti-Japanese base areas. But it does not necessarily follow that, having come to the base areas, they have already integrated themselves completely with the masses of the people here. The two must be completely integrated if we are to push ahead with our revolutionary work. The purpose of our meeting today is precisely to ensure that literature and art fit well into the whole revolutionary machine as a component part, that they operate as powerful weapons for uniting and educating the people and for attacking and destroying the enemy, and that they help the people fight the enemy with one heart and one mind. What are the problems that must be solved to achieve this objective? I think they are the problems of the class stand of the writers and artists, their attitude, their audience, their work and their study. . . .

What then is the crux of the matter? In my opinion, it consists fundamentally of the problems of working for the masses and how to work for the masses. Unless these two problems are solved, or solved properly, our writers and artists will be ill-adapted to their environment and their tasks and will come up against a series of difficulties from without and within. . . .

The first problem is: literature and art for whom?

This problem was solved long ago by Marxists, especially by Lenin. As far back as 1905 Lenin pointed out emphatically that our literature and art should "serve . . . the millions and tens of millions of working people". For comrades engaged in literary and artistic work in the anti-Japanese base areas it might seem that this problem is already solved and needs no further discussion. Actually, that is not the case. Many comrades have not found a clear solution. Consequently their sentiments, their works, their actions and their views on the guiding principles for literature and art have inevitably been more or less at variance with the needs of the masses and of the practical struggle. Of course, among the numerous men of culture, writers, artists and other literary and artistic workers engaged in the great struggle for liberation together with the Communist Party and the Eighth Route and New Fourth Armies, a few may be careerists who are with us only temporarily, but the overwhelming majority are working energetically for the common cause. By relying on these comrades, we have achieved a great deal in our literature, drama, music and fine arts. Many of these writers and artists have begun their work since the outbreak of the War of Resistance; many others did much revolutionary work before the war, endured many hardships and influenced broad masses of the people by their activities and works. Why do we say, then, that even among these comrades there are some who have not reached a clear solution of the problem of whom literature and art are for? Is it conceivable that there are still some who maintain that revolutionary literature and art are not for the masses of the people but for the exploiters and oppressors?

Indeed literature and art exist which are for the exploiters and oppressors. Literature and art for the landlord class are feudal literature and art. Such were the literature and art of the ruling class in China's feudal era. To this day such literature and art still have considerable influence in China. Literature and art for the bourgeoisie are bourgeois literature and art. People like Liang Shih-chiu [who openly criticized revolutionary art] . . . talk about litera-ture and art as transcending classes, but in fact they uphold bour-geois literature and art and oppose proletarian literature and art. Then literature and art exist which serve the imperialists—for ex-ample, the works of Chou Tsojen, Chang Tzu-ping and their like [who surrendered to the will of the Japanese invaders]—which we call traitor literature and art. With us, literature and art are for the people, not for any of the above groups. We have said that China's new culture at the present stage is an anti-imperialist, anti-feudal culture of the masses of the people under the leadership of the pro-letariat. Today, anything that is truly of the masses must necessar-ily be led by the proletariat. Whatever is under the leadership of the bourgeoisie cannot possibly be of the masses. Naturally, the same applies to the new literature and art which are part of the new cul-ture. We should take over the rich legacy and the good traditions in literature and art that have been handed down from past ages in China and foreign countries, but the aim must still be to serve the masses of the people. Nor do we refuse to utilize the literary and artistic forms of the past, but in our hands these old forms, re-moulded and infused with new content, also become something revolutionary in the service of the people.

Mao Zedong, "Talks at Yenan Forum on Literature and Art," in *Selected Works of Mao Tse-Tung*, vol. 3. Peking: Foreign Languages Press, 1967.

DOCUMENT 6: THE PROGRESS OF COMMUNISM IN CHINA

On June 30, 1949, Mao Zedong gave a speech commemorating the twenty-eighth anniversary of the founding of the Chinese Commu-nist Party. In the speech, he promised that the revolution would lead to the death of classes, state power, and political parties. China, he claimed, would then enter into a state of "Great Harmony," a con-cept long-valued by the Chinese people.

The first of July 1949 marks the fact that the Communist Party of China has already lived through twenty-eight years. Like a man, a political party has its childhood, youth, manhood and old age. The Communist Party of China is no longer a child or a lad in his teens but has become an adult. When a man reaches old age, he will die; the same is true of a party. When classes disappear, all instruments of class struggle—parties and the state machinery—will lose their function, cease to be necessary, therefore gradually wither away and end their historical mission; and human society will move to a higher stage. We are the opposite of the political parties of the bour-geoisie. They are afraid to speak of the extinction of classes, state power and parties. We, on the contrary, declare openly that we are striving hard to create the very conditions which will bring about their extinction. The leadership of the Communist Party and the state power of the people's dictatorship are such conditions. Anyone who does not recognize this truth is no communist. Young comrades who have not studied Marxism-Leninism and have only recently joined the Party may not yet understand this truth. They must understand it—only then can they have a correct world outlook. They must understand that the road to the abolition of classes, to the abolition of state power and to the abolition of parties is the road all mankind must take; it is only a question of time and conditions. Communists the world over are wiser than the bourgeoisie, they understand the laws governing the existence and development of things, they understand dialectics and they can see farther. The bourgeoisie does not welcome this truth because it does not want to be overthrown. To be overthrown is painful and is unbearable to contemplate for those overthrown, for example, for the Kuomintang reactionaries whom we are now overthrowing and for Japanese imperialism which we together with other peoples overthrew some time ago. But for the working class, the labouring people and the Communist Party the question is not one of being overthrown, but of working hard to create the conditions in which classes, state power and political parties will die out very naturally and mankind will enter the realm of Great Harmony.

Mao Zedong, "On the People's Democratic Dictatorship," in *Selected Works of Mao Tse-Tung*, vol. 4. Peking: Foreign Languages Press, 1975.

DOCUMENT 7: DICTATORSHIP AND THE LIMITS OF FREE EXPRESSION

Mao Zedong needed creative input from Chinese intellectuals so that he could foster the nation's economic development. He launched the Hundred Flowers Campaign to encourage criticism and comments from the intelligentsia. But mindful that only a year before Hungarians had rebelled against their Soviet masters, Mao gave this carefully worded speech on February 27, 1957. In it, he promotes the value of freer expression but makes it clear at the same time that it is possible to go too far.

Our state is a people's democratic dictatorship led by the working class and based on the worker-peasant alliance. What is this dictatorship for? Its first function is internal, namely, to suppress the reactionary classes and elements and those exploiters who resist the socialist revolution, to suppress those who try to wreck our socialist construction, or in other words, to resolve the contradictions between ourselves and the internal enemy. For instance, to arrest, try and sentence certain counter-revolutionaries, and to deprive landlords and bureaucrat-capitalists of their right to vote and their freedom of speech for a certain period of time—all this comes within the scope of our dictatorship. To maintain public order and safeguard the interests of the people, it is necessary to exercise dictatorship as well over thieves, swindlers, murderers, arsonists, criminal gangs and other scoundrels who seriously disrupt public order. The second function of the dictatorship is to protect our country from subversion and possible aggression by external enemies. In such contingencies, it is the task of this dictatorship to resolve the contradiction between ourselves and the external enemy. The aim of this dictatorship is to protect all our people so that they can devote themselves to peaceful labour and make China a socialist country with modern industry, modern agriculture and modern science and culture. Who is to exercise this dictatorship? Naturally, the working class and the entire people under its leadership. Dictatorship does not apply within the ranks of the people. The people cannot exercise dictatorship over themselves, nor must one section of the people oppress another. Law-breakers among the people will be punished according to law, but this is different in principle from the exercise of dictatorship to suppress enemies of the people. What applies among the people is democratic centralism. Our Constitution lays it down that citizens of the People's Republic of China enjoy freedom of speech, the press, assembly, association, procession, demonstration, religious belief, and so on. Our Constitution also provides that the organs of state must practise democratic centralism, that they must rely on the masses and that their personnel must serve the people Our socialist democracy is the broadest kind of democracy, such as is not to be found in any bourgeois state. Our dictatorship is the people's democratic dictatorship led by the working class and based on the worker-peasant alliance. That is to say, democracy operates within the ranks of the people, while the working class, uniting with all others enjoying civil rights, and in the first place with the peasantry enforces dictatorship over the reactionary classes and elements and all those who resist socialist transformation and oppose socialist construction. By civil rights, we mean, politically, the rights of freedom and democracy.

But this freedom is freedom with leadership and this democracy is democracy under centralized guidance, not anarchy. Anarchy does not accord with the interests or wishes of the people. . . .

"Let a hundred flowers blossom, let a hundred schools of thought contend" and "long-term coexistence and mutual supervision"—how did these slogans come to be put forward? They were put forward in the light of China's specific conditions, in recognition of the continued existence of various kinds of contradictions in socialist society and in response to the country's urgent need to speed up its economic and cultural development. Letting a hundred flowers blossom and a hundred schools of thought contend is the policy for promoting progress in the arts and sciences and a flourishing socialist culture in our land. Different forms and styles in art should develop freely and different schools in science should contend freely. We think that it is harmful to the growth of art and science if administrative measures are used to impose one particular style of art or school of thought and to ban another. Questions of right and wrong in the arts and sciences should be settled through free discussion in artistic and scientific circles and through practical work in these fields. They should not be settled in an over-simple manner. A period of trial is often needed to determine whether something is right or wrong. Throughout history, at the outset new and correct things often failed to win recognition from the majority of people and had to develop by twists and turns through struggle. Often, correct and good things were first regarded not as fragrant flowers but as poisonous weeds. Copernicus' theory of the solar system and Darwin's theory of evolution were once dismissed as erroneous and had to win out over bitter opposition. Chinese history offers many similar examples. In a socialist society, the conditions for the growth of the new are radically different from and far superior to those in the old society. Nevertheless, it often happens that new, rising forces are held back and sound ideas stifled. Besides, even in the absence of their deliberate suppression, the growth of new things may be hindered simply through lack of discernment. It is therefore necessary to be careful about questions of right and wrong in the arts and sciences, to encourage free discussion and avoid hasty conclusions. We believe that such an attitude will help ensure a relatively smooth development of the arts and sciences.

Mao Zedong, "On the Correct Handling of Contradictions Among the People," in *Selected Works of Mao Tse-Tung*, vol. 5. Peking: Foreign Languages Press, 1975.

DOCUMENT 8: BOMBARD THE HEADQUARTERS

Mao was struggling to maintain political control in 1966. At that time, political views were expressed in big-character posters that were hung up in public places to announce support for a viewpoint. Nie Yuanzi, a leftist philosophy teacher at Beijing University, put up her big-character poster which severely criticized university president and Party official Lu Ping. He was identified with potential rivals to Mao, Deng Xiaoping, and Lui Shaoqi. Nie Yuanzi's poster was the most significant challenge to Party officials since the founding of the nation in 1949. Counterattacks were launched against Nie Yuanzi. Mao issued his own big-character poster in which he threw his support to Nie. "Bombard the Headquarters" was Mao's rallying cry that showed his willingness to attack the Party bureaucrats if he thought they had veered from the revolutionary path. Mao's poster is the historical document credited with initiating the most extreme phase of the Cultural Revolution.

China's first Marxist-Leninist big-character poster [a reference to the poster by Nie Yuanzi] and Commentator's article on it in *Renmin ribao [People's Daily]* are indeed superbly written! Comrades, please read them again. But in the last fifty days or so some leading comrades from the central down to the local levels have acted in a diametrically opposite way. Adopting the reactionary stand of the bourgeoisie, they have enforced a bourgeois dictatorship and struck down the surging movement of the great cultural revolution of the proletariat. They have stood facts on their head and juggled black and white, encircled and suppressed revolutionaries, stifled opinions differing from their own, imposed a white terror, and felt very pleased with themselves. They have puffed up the arrogance of the bourgeoisie and deflated the morale of the proletariat. How poisonous! Viewed in connection with the Right deviation in 1962 and the wrong tendency of 1964 which was "Left" in form but Right in essence, shouldn't this make one wide awake?

Mao Zedong, "Bombard the Headquarters," August 5, 1966, from *Wild Lily, Prairie Fire: China's Road to Democracy, Yan'an to Tian'anmen, 1942–1989*, ed. Gregor Benton and Alan Hunter. Princeton, NJ: Princeton University Press, 1995.

DOCUMENT 9: QUOTATIONS FROM CHAIRMAN MAO

Quotations were collected from Mao's many speeches and writings and published in a small book with a red plastic cover. Ardent and dedicated revolutionaries carried this book everywhere, especially during the Cultural Revolution. They studied it diligently whenever possible. The book came to be known as "The Little Red Book."

Without the efforts of the Chinese Communist Party, without the Chinese Communists as the mainstay of the Chinese people, China can never achieve independence and liberation, or industrialization and the modernization of her agriculture.

"On Coalition Government" (April 24, 1945).

The Chinese Communist Party is the core of leadership of the whole Chinese people. Without this core, the cause of socialism cannot be victorious.

Talk at the general reception for the delegates to the Third National Congress of the New-Democratic Youth League of China (May 25, 1957).

A well-disciplined Party armed with the theory of Marxism-Leninism, using the method of self-criticism and linked with the masses of the people; an army under the leadership of such a Party; a united front of all revolutionary classes and all revolutionary groups under the leadership of such a Party—these are the three main weapons with which we have defeated the enemy.

"On the People's Democratic Dictatorship" (June 30, 1949).

We must have faith in the masses and we must have faith in the Party. These are two cardinal principles. If we doubt these principles, we shall accomplish nothing.

On the Question of Agricultural Cooperation (July 31, 1955).

No political party can possibly lead a great revolutionary movement to victory unless it possesses revolutionary theory and a knowledge of history and has a profound grasp of the practical movement.

"The Role of the Chinese Communist Party in the National War" (October 1938).

Communism is at once a complete system of proletarian ideology and a new social system. It is different from any other ideological and social system, and is the most complete, progressive, revolutionary and rational system in human history. The ideological and social system of feudalism has a place only in the museum of history. The ideological and social system of capitalism has also become a museum piece in one part of the world (in the Soviet Union), while in other countries it resembles "a dying person who is sinking fast, like the sun setting beyond the western hills", and will soon be relegated to the museum. The communist ideological and social system alone is full of youth and vitality, sweeping the world with the momentum of an avalanche and the force of a thunderbolt.

"On New Democracy" (January 1940).

The socialist system will eventually replace the capitalist system; this is an objective law independent of man's will. However much the reactionaries try to hold back the wheel of history, sooner or later revolution will take place and will inevitably triumph.

"Speech at the Meeting of the Supreme Soviet of the U.S.S.R. in Celebration of the 40th Anniversary of the Great October Socialist Revolution" (November 6, 1957).

The people, and the people alone, are the motive force in the making of world history.

"On Coalition Government" (April 24, 1945).

The masses are the real heroes, while we ourselves are often childish and ignorant, and without this understanding it is impossible to acquire even the most rudimentary knowledge.

"Preface and Postscript to *Rural Surveys*" (March and April 1941).

The masses have boundless creative power. They can organize themselves and concentrate on places and branches of work where they can give full play to their energy; they can concentrate on production in breadth and depth and create more and more welfare undertakings for themselves.

Introductory note to "Surplus Labour Has Found a Way Out" (1955).

Our point of departure is to serve the people whole-heartedly and never for a moment divorce ourselves from the masses, to proceed in all cases from the interests of the people and not from one's self-interest or from the interests of a small group, and to identify our responsibility to the people with our responsibility to the leading organs of the Party.

"On Coalition Government" (April 24, 1945).

On what basis should our policy rest? It should rest on our own strength, and that means regeneration through one's own efforts. We are not alone; all the countries and people in the world opposed to imperialism are our friends. Nevertheless, we stress regeneration through our own efforts. Relying on the forces we ourselves organize, we can defeat all Chinese and foreign reactionaries.

"The Situation and Our Policy After the Victory in the War of Resistance Against Japan" (August 13, 1945).

A Communist should have largeness of mind and he should be

staunch and active, looking upon the interests of the revolution as his very life and subordinating his personal interests to those of the revolution; always and everywhere he should adhere to principle and wage a tireless struggle against all incorrect ideas and actions, so as to consolidate the collective life of the Party and strengthen the ties between the Party and the masses; he should be more concerned about the Party and the masses than about any individual, and more concerned about others than about himself. Only thus can he be considered a Communist.

"Combat Liberalism" (September 7, 1937).

At no time and in no circumstances should a Communist place his personal interests first; he should subordinate them to the interests of the nation and of the masses. Hence, selfishness, slacking, corruption, seeking the limelight, and so on, are most contemptible, while selflessness, working with all one's energy, whole-hearted devotion to public duty, and quiet hard work will command respect.

"The Role of the Chinese Communist Party in the National War" (October 1938).

Communists must be ready at all times to stand up for the truth, because truth is in the interests of the people; Communists must be ready at all times to correct their mistakes, because mistakes are against the interests of the people.

"On Coalition Government" (April 24, 1945).

Every Communist working in the mass movements should be a friend of the masses and not a boss over them, an indefatigable teacher and not a bureaucratic politician.

"The Role of the Chinese Communist Party in the National War" (October 1938).

We Communists are like seeds and the people are like the soil. Wherever we go, we must unite with the people, take root and blossom among them.

"On the Chungking Negotiations" (October 17, 1945).

Mao Zedong, *Quotations from Chairman Mao Tse-Tung.* New York: Frederick A. Praeger, 1967.

DOCUMENT 10: MAO'S POEMS

Throughout his life, Mao Zedong wrote poetry, especially when moved by significant events in his life. Here are a few of Mao's poems, with contextual information provided by Jerome Ch'en.

Chu Te and his troops arrived at Chingkang Mountain in April 1928 and soon afterwards the combined forces of Mao and Chu defeated the first KMT attack at Huangyangchieh. This was probably written after the first but before the second KMT assault in July 1928.

Chingkang Mountain

Summer 1928

At the foot of the mountain
waved our banners.

Upon its peak
  sounded our bugles and drums.
A myriad foes
  were all around us.
But we stood fast
  and gave no ground.

Our defence was strong
  as a mighty wall.
Our wills united
  to form a fortress.
From Huangyangchieh
  came the thunder of guns.
And the army of our foes
  had fled into the night!

• • •

Having crossed the Gold Sand River, the Tatu (Great Ferry) River, the Grassland, and the Min Mountain . . . Mao was now in Kansu and the junction of his troops with those from north Shensi base was in sight. This is one of his less distinguished poems.

The Long March

September 1935

The Red Army fears not the trials of the Long March
And thinks nothing of a thousand mountains and rivers.
The Wuling Ridges spread out like ripples;
The Wumeng Ranges roll like balls of clay.
Warmly are the cliffs wrapped in clouds
  and washed by the Gold Sand;
Chilly are the iron chains lying across
  the width of the Great Ferry.
A thousand acres of snow on the Min Mountains delight
My troops who have just left them behind.

• • •

Shaoshan is Mao's native village, where he had led the peasants to form associations and fight for better living conditions from their landlords, before he was forced to flee in the summer of 1927.

Return to Shaoshan

June 1959

On 25 June 1959 I returned to Shaoshan, after an absence of thirty-two years.

I curse the time that has flowed past
  Since the dimly-remembered dream of my departure
From home, thirty-two years ago.

With red pennons, the peasants lifted their lances;
In their black hands, the rulers held up their whips.
Lofty emotions were expressed in self-sacrifice:
So the sun and moon were asked to give a new face to heaven.
In delight I watch a thousand waves of growing rice and beans,
And heroes everywhere going home in the smoky sunset.

Jerome Chen, *Mao and the Chinese Revolution.* New York: Oxford University Press, 1965.

DISCUSSION QUESTIONS

1. Do you agree with author Jeffrey G. Barlow that Mao's childhood was "idyllic"? What was his relationship with his father? With his mother? What kind of education did Mao receive? What was Mao's attitude toward the revolutionary movement led by Sun Yat-sen?

2. Ross Terrill says that Mao "became a spearhead for New Culture and anti-imperialism." What were some of the important ideas of the May Fourth and New Culture Movements? In what way did Mao incorporate these ideas into his own thinking, and how did he become a "spearhead," in Terrill's words?

3. After Mao left Beijing, in what types of political activity did he engage? According to Alain Bouc, what was Mao's interest in the Chinese peasantry? What was his relationship with the Nationalist Guomindang Party and with other Communists in the 1920s?

CHAPTER 2

1. Mao and his comrades living in the Jiangxi Soviet in southeastern China developed policies and principles that would stay with the Communists during their long struggle to gain power. According to J.A.G. Roberts, what were Mao's principles of guerrilla warfare? What were the three primary policies of the Communists at Jiangxi?

2. Mao biographer Dick Wilson describes some of the struggles of the Red Army as it retreated from Jiangxi with the Nationalist army on its heels. What were some of the events of the Long March, and how did the march end? How was Mao viewed by other Communists at the end of the Long March?

3. What were the principles guiding the policies of Mao and the Communists at their Yanan encampment in northern China? In what way did Mao adapt Marxism to the Chi-

nese situation? What were the principles of Communist Party control? What was the Rectification Campaign?

4. According to Jerome Chen, how did the Chinese Communist Party and the People's Liberation Army conduct their affairs during the war? How did that compare to the Nationalists? What demands did Mao make when he announced his peace terms?

CHAPTER 3

1. According to Henrietta Harrison, what were some of the problems facing the Communists in the first years of the People's Republic of China? How were these problems solved? What does Harrison say about the role of Mao as a symbol in unifying China?

2. What results did the Chinese Communists have in their attempts to improve public health, according to Dominique Hoizey and Marie-Joseph Hoizey? How did Mao respond to these results? Who were the "barefoot doctors"?

3. According to Jonathan Spence, what were the reasons for initiating the Hundred Flowers Campaign in 1957? Why do you think Mao retreated from the campaign? Based on what you read in Spence's article, do you think Mao's invitation to come forward and criticize the party's rule was a sincere desire to get help from intellectuals? What other motives might he have had?

4. Why did Mao push for the collectivization of Chinese agriculture? Based on the reading by David Curtis Wright, how would you describe the Great Leap Forward and what were the results of its policies?

5. Jonathan Spence says that Mao was "obsessed with revolutionary continuity" and the Cultural Revolution developed from this obsession. What elements were required to assure that the revolution would continue? Who were Mao's allies in this effort? According to Spence, there were two levels of violence in the Cultural Revolution. What were those two levels?

6. Maurice Meisner describes a personality cult that grew up around Mao Zedong. How did this cult originate? Did Mao resist or encourage the cult? During what era was the cult most extreme?

CHAPTER 4

1. Edward J. Lazzerini describes the ways that Deng Xiaoping's policies and ideas differed from Mao Zedong's. In what area was there the most significant policy difference

between Mao and Deng? On what issues did Deng and Mao agree?

2. Describe the accomplishments of Mao's regime, according to Maurice Meisner. How did Mao's rule affect the overall standard of living of the Chinese people?

3. Jonathan Mirsky soundly condemns Mao Zedong. What are some of Mao's destructive and ruinous policies, according to Mirsky? Explain how the Communist Party assessed Mao after his death.

4. According to Philip Short, how does Mao compare to other world leaders of his time? Why did Mao compare himself to China's first emperor, Qin Shihuangdi? Why does Short think that Mao was in a different category than other twentieth-century leaders?

Chronology

1911

Rebellion against Qing dynasty breaks out.

1912

The Republic of China is established and the last Qing emperor abdicates.

1912–1916

Yuan Shikai serves as president of the Republic of China.

1916–1927

China is controlled by regional warlords.

1919

Nations taking part in the Versailles conference in France allow Japan to control China's Shandong province. The decision sparks protests in China on May 4. The resulting May Fourth Movement and New Culture Movement bolster Chinese nationalism and advocate education, science, and rejections of traditional Confucian values.

1921

The Chinese Communist Party is founded in Shanghai.

1924

The First Congress of the Nationalist Party (Guomindang) is held.

1927

The international Communist organization (Comintern) orders the Autumn Harvest uprising against a local landlord in China. Mao Zedong is chosen to lead the rebellion. The uprising fails, and Mao and his forces retreat to the mountains.

1927–1928

Nationalist Party leader Chiang Kai-shek massacres Chinese Communists and leftist Guomindang party members.

1929

Mao Zedong and Zhu De build a base in the rural Jiangxi region and establish a Communist society there.

1930–1934

Chiang Kai-shek initiates five "extermination" campaigns against Jiangxi Communists.

1931–1932

The Japanese military seizes Manchuria and establishes a puppet state called Manchukuo.

1934–1935

Chinese Communists escape Chiang Kai-shek's fifth attack and retreat in the Long March to Yanan in the Shaanxi province. The march is over six thousand miles long and takes nearly one year.

1937

Japan invades China and launches all-out war. The rape and murder of Nanjing citizens is committed by Japanese troops in December. As many as three hundred thousand civilians are murdered. The Sino-Japanese War will last through the end of World War II in 1945.

1941

The Rectification Movement begins in Yanan. Mao requires all party members to follow his "Mao Zedong Thought."

1945

Japan is defeated and World War II ends.

1945–1947

A civil war is fought between Nationalists (Guomindang) and Communists in China.

1949

Communists win the civil war and control mainland China. The Nationalists, led by Chiang Kai-shek, flee to the island of Taiwan. Mao Zedong declares the establishment of the People's Republic of China.

1950

Communist China signs a friendship treaty with the Soviet Union. North Korea invades South Korea; the United Nations sends troops into Korea to fight for the democratic south; Chinese Communist troops enter the Korean War to aid the North Korean Communists. In China, the Marriage Law is announced, giving civil rights to Chinese women.

1951

Chinese troops enter Tibet and take over the region.

1953

China initiates its first five-year economic restructuring plan based on Soviet models.

1957

The Hundred Flowers Campaign is launched and intellectuals are encouraged to speak out and criticize the Communist Party; this free speech era is quickly followed by the Anti-Rightist Campaign in which many intellectuals are arrested and jailed. The Great Leap Forward is initiated. Farms are collectivized and industry promoted.

1959

China suppresses Tibetan rebellion. The Dalai Lama flees Tibet.

1959–1962

China suffers from famine due to the failure of the Great Leap Forward agricultural policies. Some 20 to 40 million Chinese die of starvation.

1960

China and the Soviet Union end their friendship arrangement. Soviet advisers leave China.

1964

China conducts its first nuclear tests.

1966

Mao Zedong launches the Cultural Revolution by publishing a political poster supporting leftist radicals. His intent is to return China to his own vision of the revolutionary path.

1966–1976

The Great Proletarian Cultural Revolution plunges China into chaos.

1971

Lin Biao plots to assassinate Mao; the plan fails and Lin dies (perhaps murdered) as he flees from China. Nationalist Taiwanese representatives are expelled from the United Nations and representatives from the People's Republic of China replace them.

1972

U.S. president Richard Nixon visits China.

1975

Chiang Kai-shek dies in Taiwan.

1976

Zhou Enlai, prime minister of China, dies in January. Mao Zedong dies in September. The Gang of Four members who led the Cultural Revolution are arrested.

1977

Deng Xiaoping takes control of the People's Republic of China.

FOR FURTHER RESEARCH

WRITINGS OF MAO ZEDONG

Mao Zedong, *Quotations from Chairman Mao Tse-Tung.* Ed. Stuart R. Schram. New York: Frederick A. Praeger, 1967.

———, *Selected Works of Mao Tse-Tung.* 5 vols. Beijing: Foreign Languages Press, 1977.

Stuart R. Schram, ed., *Mao's Road to Power: Revolutionary Writings.* London: M.E. Sharpe, 1992.

BIOGRAPHICAL WORKS ON MAO ZEDONG

Dennis Bloodworth, *The Messiah and the Mandarins: Mao Tsetung and the Ironies of Power.* New York: Atheneum, 1982.

Alain Bouc, *Mao Tse-Tung: A Guide to His Thought.* New York: St. Martin's Press, 1977.

Sean Breslin, *Mao.* New York: Addison Wesley Longman, 1998.

Jerome Chen, *Mao and the Chinese Revolution.* New York: Oxford University Press, 1965.

Eric Chou, *Mao Tse-tung: The Man and the Myth.* New York: Stein and Day, 1982.

Lee Feigon, *Mao: A Reinterpretation.* Chicago: Ivan R. Dee, 2002.

Stanley Karnow, *Mao and China: From Revolution to Revolution.* New York: Viking, 1976.

Li Zhisui, *The Private Life of Chairman Mao: The Memoirs of Mao's Personal Physician.* New York: Random House, 1994.

Maurice Meisner, *Mao's China: A History of the People's Republic.* New York: Free Press, 1977.

————, *Marxism, Maoism, and Utopianism: Eight Essays.* Madison: University of Wisconsin Press, 1982.

Robert Payne, *Mao Tse-tung.* New York: Weybright and Talley, 1969.

Harrison E. Salisbury, *The New Emperors: China in the Era of Mao and Deng.* Boston: Little, Brown, 1992.

Stuart R. Schram, *Mao Tse-tung.* New York: Simon & Schuster, 1966.

Philip Short, *Mao: A Life.* New York: Henry Holt, 1999.

Jonathan Spence, *Mao Zedong.* New York: Penguin Putnam, 1999.

Rebecca Stefoff, *Mao Zedong: Founder of the People's Republic of China.* Brookfield, CT: Millbrook Press, 1996.

Ross Terrill, *Mao: A Biography.* New York: Harper, 1980.

Dick Wilson, *Mao, the People's Emperor.* New York: Doubleday, 1980.

HISTORIES OF CHINA INCLUDING THE MAOIST ERA

Jasper Becker, *Hungry Ghosts: Mao's Secret Famine.* New York: Free Press, 1997.

Gregor Benton and Alan Hunter, eds., *Wild Lily, Prairie Fire: China's Road to Democracy, Yan'an to Tian'anmen, 1942–1989.* Princeton, NJ: Princeton University Press, 1995.

Marc Blecher, *China Against the Tides: Restructuring Through Revolution, Radicalism, and Reform.* London: Printer, 1997.

June Grasso, Jay Corrin, and Michael Kort, *Modernization and Revolution in China.* Armonk, NY: M.E. Sharpe, 1997.

Henrietta Harrison, *China.* London: Arnold, 2001.

Michael G. Kort, *China Under Communism.* Brookfield, CT: Millbrook Press, 1994.

Edward J. Lazzerini, *The Chinese Revolution.* Westport, CT: Greenwood Press, 1999.

J.A.G. Roberts, *Modern China: An Illustrated History.* Gloucestershire, UK: Sutton, 1998.

Harrison E. Salisbury, *The Long March: The Untold Story.* London: PanBooks, 1986.

R. Keith Schoppa, *The Columbia Guide to Modern Chinese History.* New York: Columbia University Press, 2000.

Edgar Snow, *The Long Revolution.* New York: Random House, 1972.

———, *Red Star over China.* New York: Grove Press, 1968.

Jonathan D. Spence, *Gate of Heavenly Peace: The Chinese and Their Revolution, 1895–1980.* New York: Penguin Books, 1981.

———, *The Search for Modern China.* New York: W.W. Norton, 1990.

David C. Wright, *The History of China.* Westport, CT: Greenwood Press, 2001.

WEBSITES

BBC News, China: Fifty Years of Communism, http://news. bbc.co.uk. The site, run by the British Broadcasting Corporation, has a brief biography of Mao and includes an audio link to Mao proclaiming the establishment of the People's Republic of China. There are links to other historical figures, events, and concepts in modern Chinese history.

China Online, http://chineseculture.about.com. This site, operated by About, Inc., has links to Mao's writings, information on Mao badges, posters from the Cultural Revolution, and more. There are also links to many topics related to Chinese culture: antiques, feng shui, folktales, martial arts, opera, people, a travel guide, etc.

The Mao Tse-tung (Zedong) Internet Library, www. marx2mao.org. An extensive collection of Mao's writings from 1926 to 1966 can be found at this site. There are also links to other Marxists writers: Lenin, Marx and Engels, and Stalin.

The Mao Zedong Reference Archive, www.marxists.org. This site has a biography and photos of Mao as well as many of his most important writings presented in chronological order. The site is part of the Marxist Internet Archive, including "writers whose work contributes in some way to an understanding of Marxism."

INDEX